NELLIJA'S JO

By Nellija Stonestreet

FOREWORD

Every painful experience is a lesson in life and every lesson changes a person.

I want to be sixteen again, so I can ruin my life in all sorts of different ways from what I did before. I have lots of new ideas!

CHAPTER ONE

My earliest memories...

This is what I remember. I am maybe four or five. My mother and father are at work and I am left alone in this flat all day, with no food, no toys, perhaps a pencil or a crayon to scribble on a book or magazine or sometimes the walls, for which I will be punished when my mother finds out later. We have a kitchen and a toilet. I am in the only other room which is very small. There is my parents' bed, a wardrobe, a mirror, a table and chairs and next to a high window, my bed. The window is half a metre high, I climb on my bed and then up on to the window sill to look out. Below, there are some children playing, boys and girls older than me. I am wearing only a short top and no knickers. They look up and see me and start pointing and laughing at what they see, and I have no idea why, except I know it upsets me and I start crying.

I am not at school yet; schooling in Latvia does not begin until you are seven or eight and because my birthday falls after the start of the school year, when the time comes I will be held back another year until I can start. My mother comes home after 3pm. She works as a dental technician. As soon as she gets home she has to start preparing a dinner for my father, who will be home at about 5 o'clock. He works in the construction industry, driving a bulldozer, transporting earth and rubble from one site to another and levelling the ground. One day my mother and I go to where he works to bring him some food. It is a dangerous job, with often very steep hills to level, but he drinks a lot, even when he is working and when he comes home, my mother and I are always very anxious what kind of state he will be in. We dread him coming home because he is often drunk and aggressive and kicks the door open in his rage, swearing and ranting at us. I often hide under the bed or in the toilet as he attacks my mother, verbally and physically. He demands that she go out and buy him some drink, but she has no money and has to borrow from a neighbour, who also has a husband of similar behaviour. Eventually he drinks himself to sleep and although my mother and I are relieved, we are afraid to breathe for fear of disturbing him and setting off another cycle of violence and abuse. We tiptoe around him, grateful for the relief from his frightening behaviour. My mother has discussed this situation at work. She cannot divorce him or leave him, where would she go, how would she survive? I find out later that she adopted the temporary remedy of slipping a sleeping pill in his drink; this worked for a few months but eventually the effects wore off and it was back to normal.

I was very unhappy. I remember I had a red beret and I used to bury my head in it for comfort, close my eyes and wish he was dead. I used to picture him in his coffin and felt a great sense of relief that we were free of his cruelty and violence. Even now I cannot feel guilty nor have regret about these feelings, such was the level of fear and dread that he made me feel. One Christmas we were waiting for him to come home with his wages so that my mother could go out and buy some Christmas provisions. My aunt worked at the shop where we would go for this and he was late, time was getting on, it was dark and the shop was due to close at 5.30pm. As the shop was close to the route he would take to come home, my mother and I went to meet him. There was a level crossing near to the shop and we waited in the darkness as a train was about to pass. As it did there was the sound of a collision, the train alarm sounded and in the lamplight I could see a man, to my horror, my father, staggering towards me, whose fingers on one hand had been severed with just the veins hanging from where the fingers had been. He had apparently passed out through drink by the railway track and was very lucky that it was only his fingers that were lost. He was taken to hospital and lost three fingers, including one that the surgeons tried to sew back on but failed.

When sober, my father was a different man. Originally from Smolensk in Russia, he had been moved to Latvia with his family during the war as a child, being about five at the time. My mother was Latvian, born in Madona, where she lived all her life. She had never loved my father, only marrying him because she became pregnant with me, which is what you had to do in those days. He, on the other hand, was in love with her and called her his squirrel, a Russian form of endearment. When I was born, he came to the hospital with a gift that he had made for my mother consisting of a brand of chocolates called 'Squirrel' in their wrappers which he had bound together to form a bow on which he had inscribed 'To my squirrel'.

At home my parents spoke Russian and naturally that was the first language I learned to speak. However, my mother's family only spoke Latvian, and as we saw a lot of them, I picked up that language quickly as well. It all seemed perfectly normal to me at the time which shows how easily a young child can learn, even informally. The different languages often caused trouble between the two sides of my family and gatherings of both sides almost always ended in rows as each side resolutely refused to even allow the other side to speak in their own language. My paternal grandmother, from whom I fear I have unfortunately inherited some of her least desirable characteristics such as a very volatile temperament, was particularly vocal in her insistence on speaking Russian and there were many occasions when my father, in support of my mother, had to ask his parents to leave our house in the middle of a big row, which was always upsetting and distressful to a young child. Unlike his mother, my maternal grandmother was a quiet, kind and thoughtful lady who was always there to comfort and reassure me. This loving nature was something lacking in both my parents. Without wanting to sound full of self pity, I never felt really loved by either of them. Neither was demonstrative, I was never told anything nice about myself, never had a cuddle or a hug and we never ever had that close, affectionate bond that you hope parents might have with their children.

Despite his terrible behaviour when he was drunk, I do have some happy memories of my father when he was sober. As a family, myself, my father and mother and my maternal grandparents used to spend a lot of time in the forests that surround Madona. It is a national pastime in Latvia to forage for mushrooms, and the forests contain an abundance of them with many different varieties, all free to pick, take home, prepare and eat in a whole range of different ways. We would spend many happy hours gathering them and my father taught me all the different names and which ones you could eat and which ones were poisonous. How he had acquired this knowledge I have no idea but I am so grateful he passed it on to me, because all my life I have had an affinity with the beautiful forests of my homeland, and particularly its mushrooms. Whenever I have felt depressed or upset, a visit to the forest would always quickly do wonders to restore my sense of well being. There is something magical and life affirming about the smell, the solitude, the peace and natural beauty of unspoilt woodland that is a tonic for the soul.

Some other recollections of my early childhood include being allowed out to play at weekends. As I have said, I never had a doll or even a cuddly toy of any kind when I was a child so perhaps it was not surprising that I always played with boys rather than girls. I was usually the ringleader as we played warlike games with sticks of wood as sabres, leading my troops into battle against the enemy.
I was always adventurous and this led to another incident which saw me confined to home for a while. Close to our small block of flats, building was about to start on another block, and lorries would come and go with deliveries in preparation for the building. One day, a lorry delivered a load of tar while I watched in fascination as the black substance oozed out on to the ground, covering a wide area and forming a hill which rose to about a metre high. Of course, I wanted to climb to the top and began the ascent, but before long sunk up to my knees in the sticky warmth of the tar. I was unable to extricate myself and could feel I was

sinking in deeper, convinced I was going to die, although I also realised I would probably be killed when I got home anyway! By now I had attracted a crowd of men, women and children including my mother, but while the men stood around watching, reluctant to plunge in to save me, one brave and inventive soul came to my rescue by using some planks of wood to climb on to the heap and pull me out. I had lost my shoes and socks and was covered in tar, so when I got home I was put in the bath to clean up. This proved very difficult and my mother had to go to the builders' merchant to get some cleaning material to get rid of the mess I was in. As a result, I was kept in for a week as punishment.

On the promise of good behaviour, I was allowed out again eventually but soon got back into trouble. I had never had a bicycle and the sight of a boy riding a bike on a hilltop near to where we lived made me envious. I spoke to the boy and after long negotiations persuaded him to let me ride it for a short time. Unfortunately I got carried away with the thrill of it, forgot how to brake while careering towards the cliff edge and promptly sailed over a twenty five metre drop to the ground below. The bicycle was in pieces, I landed on my elbows and knees, there was blood everywhere and I was lucky I didn't break anything. Needless to say, my mother was furious with me and after I was treated by an ambulance crew to clean me up and bandage the cuts and grazes, she subjected me to some physical punishment which hurt more than the crash. Pulling my hair and ears were just two of her specialities and of course, I was once again confined to the flat.

My father meanwhile was continuing to drink heavily and his health was deteriorating. He went to the doctor's and was found to have two ulcers as a result of which he took notice of the warning and stopped drinking for about six months before starting up again. Later, when I was about 16 years old, tragedy struck. He was sent to buy something by his employer and was on a moped which was in collision with a large jeeplike vehicle. He was thrown from the moped, landing on the pavement but his injuries were not considered life threatening when he was taken to hospital for observation. My mother went to see him and they were walking in the hospital grounds and she left him, reassured that he was going to be alright, and would see him the next morning. The next day when she entered the ward, his bed was empty and she was told he had died. The post mortem revealed he had died as a result of damage to his Adam's Apple which the doctor in charge had initially failed to identify. My father's mother took this matter up with the authorities and the doctor lost his job, but that was little consolation for the loss of a father, husband and son who was not yet forty.

Near where we lived there was a small kiosk selling ice cream. This was a real treat for me, I could have a waffleglass, or cornet, filled with ice cream, but only once a month if I was lucky although there always seemed to be enough money for drink. I remember the waffle glass was only 2 kopeks, the ice cream was priced depending on how much you had. The shop where my aunt on my father's side worked had lots of sweets and chocolates on display but my mother never bought any for me, although I knew other children had them. I discovered my mother bought chocolates for herself and hid them in the wardrobe and I got in the habit of stealing one or two so that one day my mother noticed that stocks were low and challenged me about it. I strongly denied that I was the culprit. One day when my mother and I were in the shop my aunt asked my mother why she never bought me any sweets or chocolates but it did not change anything.

Before starting school I had a bout of rheumatic fever, which left me with a rheumatic heart condition. This resulted in me being sent to a sanatorium by the seaside in Jurmala. This was in the days when it was believed that the seaside was the cure for all ills and I was there for two or three weeks as I remember. Later, I was taken to the doctor's because my mother noticed I was very pale and I was having dizzy spells and fainting quite often. The diagnosis was anaemia and I spent two weeks in hospital on a drip to normalise my blood. On reflection, I was probably underfed and what little food I had was probably of poor quality anyway. I subsequently had two more spells at different sanatoriums during my childhood years. My most vivid memories from those times are of walking on the seashore and collecting amber, which was plentiful and easy to find at low tide. There were also plenty of jellyfish and shellfish which I remember picking up and then throwing back.

And so eventually, at eight, I was old enough to go to school, where I started off at a massive disadvantage. All of the other children had learnt their alphabet at the very least, some had been to kindergarten and could read and write. I had never been taught any of these things, left to my own devices, cooped up in a small flat day to day with no attempt to teach me anything. I didn't even know one plus one equals two. Needless to say, I was ashamed and embarrassed and very unhappy and my slowness to learn was made worse by the cruelty of my teacher, a sadistic woman who took a delight in hitting me, pinching me and even using the blackboard chalk as a weapon, apart from the verbal humiliation to which she subjected me. One day my mother noticed the bruises on my arms and I told her that the teacher had done it, which was true. When confronted by my mother, the teacher leaned over me and said 'Nelly, is it true that I did this?' and I was so frightened for fear of further violence that I said 'no'. However, after about two years of this miserable existence, everything seemed to fall into place and I began to catch up. I became an avid reader, spending most of my spare time reading books. This came about when I contracted measles and then developed conjunctivitis when I was about eleven years old. I remember being unable to open my eyes for a few days losing all sense of time and when I was recovering all I wanted was to each sweets and chocolates which I stole from the usual place! Bored and still recovering at home, I started reading a library book whose name I cannot remember, but it was about people and their contacts with the animals in the forest and I was captivated by it, not being able to put it down until I had finished it, even if that meant reading it by torchlight under my duvet during the night when my parents were asleep.

From then on, I read everything I could get my hands on from the library, first of all from the childrens' section and later at about 13 or so from the adult section. Although Madona was only a small town, it had a well equipped library including a section on international literature, which I was drawn to rather than the classic Russian novels of Dostoevsky and Tolstoy. I remember some of the names – John Galsworthy's 'Forsyte Saga', some Dickens, lots of Alexander Dumas' 'Three Musketeers', 'Count of Monte Cristo' and 'La Reine Margot' and the American writer Theodore Dreiser's 'American Tragedy' and 'Sister Carrie'. I read Margaret Mitchell's 'Gone With The Wind' readily identifying myself with the heroine Scarlett O'Hara. All in Russian of course and to prove my wide taste, just for good measure a science fiction novel by the Russian writer Alexander Belyaev, 'Professor Dowell's Head'. I seemed to spend most waking hours outside school reading and even during the night I would take a book into the toilet and sit on the seat reading for hours at a time. Eventually, it got to the stage where I had read every book in the library that I was interested in and so I had to resort to borrowing books from friends and buying from a local bookshop in order to quench my appetite.

My transformation at school from those miserable early years was complete as I excelled at reading in front of the class, taking dictation and writing précis. We were able to write our own compositions from a choice of subjects – mine were usually about holidays in Russia, close to nature among the forests and their magic. Although my main preoccupation was reading, as I got older there were other distractions, of which I knew little at the time. My best friend at school was Natalya. She and I were close although we had a little falling out when I was about ten years old. On arriving at school one morning, I found that the shelf under my desk where I usually put my books was already full and to my surprise there was a present done up with a ribbon. I opened the package and found it contained chocolates and flowers and a card from a boy named Viktor, who was in my class but of whom I was hardly aware. Natalya was very jealous of this attention but she had no reason to be as nothing developed from it. There was another boy named Gennady who I liked but tragically he later drowned in a nearby lake. Natalya and I got over that little tiff and we remained friends. She was a lot more worldly than I was. She knew about smoking, drinking and boys. One day at her house she introduced me to her mother's home made vodka, which I had never tasted before and had no idea of its potency, although I should have known better from my experiences with my father. We went to a disco that evening and I remember being much the worst for wear, and being sick most of the time.

But I am getting ahead of myself here and must go back to earlier times. For the first four years at school children were provided with warm milk and bread for a mid morning break, but in the next year things were different. Lessons began at 8am, each one lasted 45 minutes and at the end of each lesson children could buy themselves food and drink. It was up to parents to provide this money but my parents gave me nothing. I would start school not having had a breakfast and would have nothing to eat until I got home. The only drink was water from a tap in the school. School finished at 2 in the afternoon and I would go home, find the key under the front door mat and wait for my mother to come home and cook something. Occasionally one of the other children would take pity on me and offer me a bite or two of what they had. When apples were in season I would sometimes steal from trees overhanging the pavement and on another occasion I found a 50 kopek coin on the pavement with which I was able to buy something to eat.

In Madona, there was a large open air theatre which put on concerts and discos, attracting large crowds who came to listen and dance and eat and drink in the natural amphitheatre that surrounded the stage. There were market stalls selling food and drink and it was a hive of activity with events going on until the early hours of the morning. My maternal grandparents used to go back to this area after the crowds had gone and collect up all the discarded bottles for which they would collect 20 kopeks a time from a local store that took them. They did very well at this and also acquired lots of other items that people had lost in the darkness, like coins, wristwatches and earrings. They were generous to me from their spoils and every week or so gave me money which I used to buy food and drink at the school.

My clothes were another source of embarrassment and shame to me. I wore the same clothes to school every day because I had no others. By the end of the week naturally they would smell and my trousers inevitably became worn, damaged and stained, with tears and holes in them. I tried to darn and patch things up as best I could, but of course my efforts were clumsy and unprofessional. My mother as usual showed no interest and I remember my aunt on my father's side frequently remonstrated with her about my clothes but to no avail. One day, the teacher made me get up from my desk and go to the blackboard to write something and as I began to do so, there was a burst of laughter from the children because of the state of my trousers My grandparents one year bought me a winter coat for my birthday from the proceeds of their bottle collecting. The first day I wore it I was walking home from school when a group of children came running up behind me playing games and generally messing around and one boy grabbed hold of my brand new coat and in doing so, ripped all the buttons off it.

Every year, during the summer we would make a visit to my father's numerous family members in Russia, many of them living in small villages deep in the forest land of his birth, where his people worked on farms, with animals or with crops. I remember these times with fondness, the hospitality was warm and inviting, the fresh country air was invigorating and it was a million miles away from the confinement and deprivations of my life in that small flat in Madona. For about a year, I had suffered from a recurring problem with styes - one would clear up in one eye only for my other eye to develop a new one, and so it went on. They were very painful, apart from the social embarrassment. One day during one of our breaks in Russia, an old lady, I am not sure if she was a relative of my father or not, noticed this problem and promptly took me outside, told me to close my eyes and turn round to face her, where upon she threw a scattering of chicken feed in my face. The next day, as promised, the stye had cleared up and I never had the problem again. Since that day, rightly or wrongly, I have always had a healthy respect for peasant folklore and remedies. Thinking back, we probably went to Russia most years when I was between the ages of 6 and 15. When I was 14 my parents decided that that year I could stay on with my father's family during the school holidays, which started early and finished late, so I had the best part of three months there. I loved it, and remember every morning having a drink of half a litre of warm cow's milk fresh from the udder. The food, the outdoors and everything about their way of life did me good, and when my parents came to collect me at the end of the holidays they could hardly recognise the healthy looking, well developed girl I had become compared to the skinny, sickly, pale child they had left behind. For my part, when they came to collect me I remember seeing them in the garden and thinking that they were strangers to me, two people I hardly knew and felt little towards. My time that summer was idyllic, with warm, kind people who were good to each other and despite the hard work, full of life and fun. During these years I met the first love of my life, a village boy called Ivan. We would go for long walks together, have deep and meaningful conversations and never even so much as kissed but we had a strong affinity and we would write to each other every week once I was back home. This was before sex had been invented in Russia and Latvia and I was a complete innocent about the facts of life!

The year my father died, my mother and I were invited to spend Christmas in Russia with his family and the festivities were in full swing when we got there, with the adults grouped together in one house and the young people in another. Music was playing, drinks were plentiful and I remember being offered a large glass of cognac which I declined. At night we all slept together in a communal area, and I was happy to be with Ivan again. He was due to go into the army on national service late next year and we started talking about making plans to get married when this was finished after two years.

CHAPTER TWO

Back in Madona the next year I started going to discos with girl friends from my class. At that time, girls waited to be asked to dance and I received many invitations from various boys, the most frequent a young man named Vladimir. We danced together most weeks and eventually this developed into him walking home with me, then he would turn up under our flat window with presents like a cuddly toy animal. One weekend I had a birthday party invitation to a village some way from Madona and he offered to take me on his moped. The party went on into the late evening, too late to go home and we were offered to stay the night in a hay barn near the main house. I was a girl of seventeen who had never had the basic facts of life explained to me by either my mother or a teacher at school, who had never even been kissed by a man before and I had no idea of what was happening until it was too late and in any case I could not stop him as he forced himself upon me. The next morning when I got home I was greeted at the door by a slap from my mother before I had a chance to explain, which made it impossible for me to tell her what had happened. As the weeks went by my worst fears were that I was pregnant so eventually I went to the local hospital where it was confirmed that I was indeed pregnant with twins. I did not want to go through with the pregnancy and arranged an abortion. This was carried out with great difficulty, I had to undergo two operations during which my temperature became dangerously high at over 40 degrees. Vladimir had been delighted with the news that he was to become a father and was of course very upset at the abortion but I knew it was the right thing to do. However, I agreed to marry him as my reputation in a small town where gossip spreads quickly was likely to be ruined unless I stuck with him, so arrangements were made that we would get married in November of that year, 1977, two months after I turned 18. On the day of the wedding, one hour after the ceremony but before the reception, my mother showed me a telegram she had received a couple of days before from Ivan. It read that he was about to go in the army and would I go to see him before he went so that we could plan our future together. Had I known about this before the wedding my life could have been so different and I will never know how things might have turned out. All I know is that I was robbed of the chance to begin a new life with the boy I really loved, who had always treated me with love and respect and never once tried to take advantage of me.

I soon found out what sort of character my husband was. He was coarse in his language and behaviour, had no regard for personal hygiene or cleanliness at all and was generally a gross, disgusting and repulsive person. I discovered that while at school he had had an accident, falling from some height on to a concrete floor and landing on his head, which had made him unfit for military service and had probably caused some kind of brain damage. The story went that he had bribed a police officer to obtain a driving licence as he certainly would not have been able to pass a test. Although all this seemed to be common knowledge in the town, I only became aware of it when it was too late.

Married life began in a council flat, one of five in an old wooden building that probably dated back to before the war. More like a barn than a house, water had to be obtained from a pump in the yard. The flat was one small room plus a kitchen with a wood burning stove. Conditions were squalid. The toilet was shared with all the other occupants of the house and was outside, some fifty metres away from the house. It was extremely unpleasant in the summer and even worse in the winter for different reasons. He worked as a delivery driver for small wages while I had a good job with an electrical manufacturer in the town, working on an assembly line dealing with lamps and other electrical accessories.

We had some rabbit hutches outside with more than 200 rabbits. The skins could be sold at around 5 roubles each. We used to nail the skins to a plywood board to stretch and dry them before selling them to a local dealer and this helped to supplement our income. Unfortunately we were plagued with rats and our neighbour put down some rat poison to try to get rid of them. This led to the drinking water for the rabbits being infected and the adult rabbits died as a result. This led to the baby rabbits not being fed by their mothers with most of them subsequently dying as well. This horror caused me nightmares for many years, a recurring dream that I had forgotten to feed my rabbits for three days and they had all died. This dream was always the same and was so vivid it was probably the best part of 30 years before these nightmares stopped.

When I discovered I was pregnant I was very unhappy as I did not want a baby, I did not love my husband and felt trapped in a situation from which there seemed no escape. The daily drudgery continued – carrying heavy buckets of water from the pump, chopping up and bringing in the firewood - before or after my job. Neighbours would comment on this to him, but he just shrugged it off as my choice although he never lifted a finger to help me. I began to accept this life for what it was, a life where there was no place for love or kindness, much the same as my parents had lived. There was a small ray of hope however. After seven months of my pregnancy I was able to take maternity leave up to a month after the birth of what turned out to be my first daughter. The money was good, 250 roubles a month so I was expecting to be able to buy all the necessary items for the impending birth, such as a pram, a cot and baby clothes. My husband had other ideas and took the money I had earned and saved to buy himself a motor bike and sidecar without consulting me.

I had a difficult time when my daughter was born in March 1978. She weighed 4½ kilos and the placenta became lodged, necessitating an operation to remove it. After a week we were allowed to return home. One day I went shopping leaving him with the baby and happened to bump into a woman I knew but hadn't seen for some time. We got talking and she told me something that shocked me deeply. On the day that our daughter was born, Vladimir had come into her office and given a bunch of flowers to one of the girls who worked there, in appreciation of their previous night together apparently. It was also common knowledge that he would bed anyone he could, again, something I was not previously aware of. When I got home in a state of complete shock I challenged him about this particular girl and he hotly denied it, claiming that people were jealous of our life together and trying to make trouble out of nothing.

Liana, our daughter was crying incessantly day and night and could not be comforted. It was discovered that she had an umbilical hernia and also that my milk was of poor quality and not providing her with sufficient nutrition, so a supplement was prescribed. Vladimir had no patience with her and one day when she was especially unhappy, he bundled me out of the house, locked the door and stormed off, leaving her alone in the flat to cry. My fault of course because I pampered her too much. In the meantime we had moved to a slightly bigger flat in the same building but then Liana developed a bacterial skin infection. She was hospitalised in an isolation ward and because I was still breastfeeding her I went as well. At this time, my husband's grandmother died and I was expected, indeed obliged, to go to her funeral. As I was still weaning my daughter, I received special permission to leave the hospital on condition I would return that evening. Predictably, after the funeral, at the wake Vladimir became drunk and I realised I would have to catch the last bus to get back to the hospital. During the evening, his drunken behaviour got worse and he violently attacked me, punching and striking me in the face. This vicious assault resulted in two black eyes, a split and swollen lip and numerous bruises, in which state I had to endure a painful, embarrassing bus journey back to the hospital. The next morning he turned up at the hospital and although he was not allowed in as it was an isolation ward, he came to the window and when he saw my face, started laughing at me in great amusement at what he had done, which was a good example of the kind of character he was.

I was becoming used to and accepting of his violent behaviour and foolishly when we were allowed to come home, I reverted to the old routine. Although I was still recovering from the difficult birth of Liana and her subsequent problems, Vladimir again forced himself on me without regard for my weak physical and mental state and I became pregnant again. Arranging for either of my grandmothers or his mother to care for my daughter, I went back to work again for a few months as money was tight and there were always bills to be paid. My son Sergei was born in April of 1979 and this was the first moment my maternal instincts were aroused when I held him in my arms and felt a deep love for him. This was something I had never felt when my daughter was born. Vladimir was also delighted, so much so that he gave me a gold ring with a ruby inset which must have cost about three or four months average wages at that time. I had no idea where he got the money for it, probably his mother, but I was happy to wear it. This temporary respite in a life of hardship soon came to an end.

It was summer evening, probably about seven o'clock so still light. I was at home with the children while Vladimir had gone out for some shopping. My uncle on my mother's side called by and I invited him in for a coffee. However, it was not a social visit. He told me that he had seen my husband's motor bike outside the flat of a notorious woman who was known to receive many male visitors. I immediately dressed – I had bought a new jumper that same day which was the first item of clothing to hand, and made my way to the flat. I rang the bell, she answered and I asked to speak to my husband. He came to the door and I told him to come home. He did not have the sidecar with the bike so I had to ride pillion. There was only one helmet, which he was going to wear so I had no headgear. He drove like a madman and deliberately steered into some debris on the roadside which threw me off the bike on to the road, landing on my head. He carried on home. Fortunately, where the accident, if you can call it that, happened was outside of my doctor's house. She heard the commotion and came out and I was carried into the house and wrapped up in a towel as my head was bleeding profusely, and eventually an ambulance arrived to take me to the hospital. There was no spare bed there so I spent the night in a corridor but in the operating theatre I had stitches to close an 11 centimetre gash in my head. I was concussed, badly bruised, both eyes swollen so badly I could not open them and an xray revealed hairline bone fractures which have resulted in never ending spinal problems ever since. After three days Vladimir came to see me, bringing me a watermelon as a peace offering and pleading with me to say that I had been driving the bike, as he would be in big trouble when the accident was investigated. The next day a police officer came to the hospital to interview me and I signed a statement in which I stated that I was the driver. I spent two weeks in hospital and returned home, again back to the usual routine of household drudgery and unhappiness.

This was a time when Soviet collective farming was still being vigorously enforced, and at times such as potato harvesting, extra workers were co-opted to help out, such as the women from the electrical factory where I had worked. One day when I was out shopping I met a woman from the factory who took great pleasure in telling me about an event which left me reeling once again. Vladimir had waylaid her when she was about to board the bus to take her to the village where the potatoes were being dug and persuaded her to let him give her a lift there instead. In the course of the journey he persuaded her to have sex with him and she insisted on recounting all the graphic details which I had no wish to hear.

On returning home my mind was made up. I needed to divorce this person and try to start a new life for myself and this was the time. A flat in the same block where his mother lived had become available and he was very keen to take it as it was larger than where we were living. I went along with this but when it came to signing the papers I told him that I wanted a divorce and was going to stay in our existing flat. The divorce proceedings were extremely protracted. It took nine months before it finally happened during which time he failed to attend a couple of court hearings in an attempt to frustrate my petition but eventually I got a letter confirming that I was now free. I was outside, getting the wood in or perhaps the water and came back, not locking the door. Suddenly, there was a kicking at the door, he burst in, drunk and shouting and in a furious rage. I had taken off my gold ring while I was working, and he, seeing this, picked it up and threw it with great force against the wall. I rushed to pick it up and saw that it was completely flattened. Next, he threw open my wardrobe and hurled some of my clothes across the room. I told him that I was going to call the police and he eventually calmed down and left.

CHAPTER 3

Back at work, a three day break in nearby Estonia was arranged for some of the workers and we set off in a bus for a welcome change of scenery. The children were left with either one set of my grandparents or Vladimir's mother, I can't exactly remember so when we got back in Madona I was expecting the flat to be empty. However, as soon as I opened the door I realised something was wrong. The first room on opening the door was the kitchen, and it had been stripped. Next, the bed and on the white sheet were dirty boot marks, black mud and whatever else where someone had climbed on to the bed and ripped from the wall the colourful, patterned mat, a wedding present, which had been nailed on there as an insulation against the cold. There were gaping holes in the wall because of the force with which the matting had been wrenched away from the plaster. It was obvious who was responsible, everything that was taken was from Vladimir's side of the family. Faced with a lack of furniture and with my children, who would be coming home soon with nowhere to sleep apart from all the other missing home comforts, my father's mother suddenly appeared and within a few hours she had managed to obtain a table, chairs and other furniture we needed so urgently and thanks to her yet another crisis was averted. She settled me down with a drink of Riga Black Balsam, a strong alcoholic drink blended with herbs, which relaxed me and I had a good night's sleep despite the traumas of earlier.

She came across Vladimir's mother the next day and told her what had happened, which shocked her greatly. I never had any problems with her, she was also very good to the children. After about a week, Vladimir paid me a visit to ask about seeing the children and he was shocked to see my new furniture. Incredibly, he maintained that his theft of the old furniture was intended as a desperate ploy to get me to go back to him. I was trying to make a new life for myself but he continued to pester me. One evening I was at home playing cards with a couple of male friends of his when he turned up and asked what they were doing there. He was politely told that it was none of his business anymore.

One of those two friends was a man named Alexander. He was quiet, kind and considerate, never lost his temper and was good with the children, who both got on well with him. We gradually began to see more of each other and I remember we would stay up all night talking until the dawn. He would come round for meals, we would go out together as a family and had some good times. He had been married but was divorced from his wife who had turned out to be an unfaithful slut, and was living with his mother. For the first time, I was beginning to enjoy a normal relationship with a man who treated me decently, far from the abuse and violence I had been subjected to with Vladimir. However, this did not sit well with my ex husband, who together with his mother, went to see Alexander's mother telling a tale of how her son was preventing a possible reconciliation between us. One evening his mother came to the flat when Alexander and I were having a meal and called on us to stop seeing each other. He tried to defuse the situation by taking her home but the damage was done, she succeeded in splitting us up as he was either unable or unwilling to stand up to her and continue seeing me.

Some while after, his mother went to see my paternal grandmother and aunt and over tea expressed her remorse for the role she had played in ending our relationship. Alexander had retreated into himself and was drinking heavily, desperately unhappy and feeling he had nothing to live for. Now she could see she was in the wrong, regretted her actions and begged my relatives to intercede on his behalf to get us back together. However, my grandmother and aunt told her that it was she must approach me direct with her son as they were not prepared to get involved. She never did, neither did he and there it finished. I saw him several times in later years and always felt a pang of regret for what might have been, if only he had been strong enough to stand up to his mother, as I never lost the feeling I had for him. Sadly, his drinking became worse and then he contracted cancer, dying long before his time. He had obviously felt for a long time he had nothing to live for and it was a sad ending to a the life of man who I still remember with love and affection. We never had a cross word and he showed me that a different life to the one I had lived thus far was possible.

In the meantime I became aware that my job at the electrical factory was getting too much for me so I decide on a change of direction. I took a brief training course and got a job in a shop selling home ware and equipment. A girl I worked with happened to mention that there was a club at a village called Sauleskalns, where they had a dance floor, refreshments and entertainment. There was a big army barracks at nearby Marcienas and many of the soldiers used to go there, according to my work colleague. It was a fair distance from Madona, about 12 kilometres, so although we might get a bus out there, getting home might involve either a long walk home or a lift from some obliging man. We went, hoping for the best and during the evening I was asked to dance by two men in particular, one of whom I liked very much and another, who I did not care for at all. When the evening came to a close, my work colleague had disappeared and so had the man I was enamoured with, but the second favourite was still in attendance so we decided to walk home together. I discovered that he was on probation in the army and that his father's family were from nearby Lubana. His father had been a fighter for the fascists during the war and was subsequently exiled to Vladivostok in far off Siberia by the Soviet regime and had married a woman from that area, Pavel being their son. Eventually we arrived in Madona after a long walk and I showed him where I worked and he said goodnight at my door and I never thought any more about it. I was surprised some days later when he turned up at the shop where I worked and asked if he could see me home when the shop closed. I still did not warm to him and took care to distance myself from him on the walk home if I saw anyone I knew.

I was fed up with the poorly paid shop job and some friends mentioned that a nearby mink farm had vacancies and paid well, so I looked into it and was soon working there. It was a vast concern, with thousands of animals housed in cages in a number of sheds. I was assigned one particular shed of about 300 mink and my job was to feed, water and clean them. Health and safety standards, not to mention animal welfare matters, were of course years in the future so I was given no protective clothing, not even gloves to deal with these vicious little animals. They were all housed in individual cages and on opening the cage, very cautiously and armed with a rake to keep them at bay, I would clean out the revolting contents. The smell was overpowering and if they got the chance they would bite you. Fortunately I was only bitten once, but had to stay off work for two weeks nonetheless. They slept on either straw, hay or sawdust, whichever happened to be in supply and their food was a kind of porridge made from meat, fish or whatever was available. I had a food trolley from which I doled out their food by hand, not even a basic ladle was provided. I remember the first day when I finished I was covered in black on my arms and legs. This turned out to be fleas, but I was assured they were not interested on humans, only the mink, so that was supposed to be all right

During the time I worked there I was seeing Pavel about once a month. He was living with his parents' family in Lubana and I believe was still on probation with the army although he was shortly to fail his medical and was released. I still did not warm to him and remember that I was glad if it was dark when we went for walks together so that as few people as possible would see us together. As the year wore on, and winter was approaching my situation was not good. The only source of heating in my flat was firewood for the stove and this was expensive. After I had paid for food for myself and the children and paid the bills there was little money left. I had to resort to taking a large wheelbarrow, more accurately a cart, and go to both sets of my grandparents and bring home what little spare wood they had for my stove. This involved long and tiring walks across town pulling the cart behind me and I began to despair for my future. I have always believed that God has a plan for all of us and I began to think that perhaps Pavel was part of the solution. He was out of work and had only the clothes that he stood up in but nevertheless he seemed to be a normal responsible man and we might have a better future so it was that we started to live together before the end of the year.

At the mink farm, December was the time of year when their fur was at its best so that was the month for slaughtering them and it was my job to go round with a vet and usher each animal into a box where the vet would administer a fatal jab. After they were all killed the next stage of the operation was to skin them. I was not involved in that but the next process was to de-grease the skin by using a special implement and this was very well paid work from which I remember I was paid 1000 Roubles over a couple of weeks. One day, Pavel was at home occupied with chores like woodchopping and cleaning the house and I was particularly late at work as the mink processing meant longer hours. By the time I finished the last bus had gone and I was faced with a long walk home in the cold and dark. However, when I got home I was pleasantly surprised to find that the flat was clean and warm and a hot dinner was ready for me, a tasty meat goulash which I enjoyed very much. I asked him about the meat and he told me that he had killed one of our remaining rabbits. Shortly after, my near neighbour Ruta called in on us. She worked at a nearby diary and used to bring home some of their products which she had stolen from the dairy, such as soured cream and which she used to share with us. On entering our flat she looked at the stove and noticed that the wood lying by it had come from their shed. They had not got a key and Pavel had helped himself thinking that they would not miss it. I was very ashamed of his actions but we said no more about it.

I had had enough of working at the mink farm, the conditions were horrible and I could never get rid of the smell. I decided to quit and a leaving party was arranged for me at a colleague's flat in Lazdona, a village near the mink farm. We were both invited and there was plenty of food and drink so the evening passed pleasantly enough but it ended with a warning that I should have taken to heart. Towards the end of the party I realised Pavel had been missing for some time and no one knew where he was. I looked for him but there was no sign, and I needed the toilet but found that it was occupied, as a woman's voice called out to go away! I ended up walking home, a very long and dangerous journey late at night on a largely unlit road with no pavement most of the way until I reached Madona. Pavel did not return until the next day and there was never an explanation but I was later to understand only too well what had happened.

Pavel had got a new job as a loader at the local flour mill, moving grain from the train to the mill, heavy work but well paid. He had a driving licence but no car and in those days you had to have evidence that you were currently driving or you lost your licence so his sympathetic boss lent him a car for a couple of weeks. One day he came home with it, full of expensive chocolates and sweets and handed me a big bag which on opening I found contained about 500 roubles. The sweets were that 'squirrel' brand so beloved by my father, which of course, went straight to my heart.

My mother had her birthday in April and we went to her flat to celebrate. At this time my mother, who had only occasionally drank, usually just to keep my father company, started to get into the habit of drinking Riesling. It developed from just a glass at a time to a bottle and then she switched to port. She had been transferred to a different job with the dental department and was now a receptionist at the hospital where she was in charge of booking appointments and responsible for taking payments from patients. Each week she had to hand over the cash and the records to the administration department and as her drinking habit increased she used to use some of this money to finance it, paying it back when she was paid. This was very worrying for me and I tried to warn her, but her dependence on alcohol was becoming too strong.

Back to her birthday. My grandparents were there and also invited was an upstairs neighbour, an older woman and her daughter, the latter someone who I knew had a reputation as being of easy virtue. As the evening wore on, mother and daughter left to go back upstairs to their flat while our family continued drinking and enjoying the time together. Pavel said he was going outside for a while and after a time I decided to go out and look for him. I searched all the downstairs area, where each flat in the block had a storage room and then went upstairs and knocked on the door of the old woman's flat. She came to the door and I asked to see her daughter and when she prevaricated, I burst past her and went from room to room and eventually the toilet, where the door was looked and a voice called out that she was busy. Despite my previous experiences with Vladimir, I realise now that I was incredibly naïve about men and far too trusting. Experience has sadly taught me otherwise but perhaps I was unlucky that I seemed to attract the unfaithful type who would have sex with anything that moved. I went back downstairs to my mother's flat and opened and closed the door, thinking that Pavel would believe I was back inside the flat but I waited outside in the corridor for him to avoid an unpleasant scene inside the flat with my relatives.

CHAPTER 4

Despite this weakness, Pavel was a decent, quiet, hard working man who was good with the children, and although they were not his, he treated them kindly and was never squeamish about feeding them, wiping their noses and all the other little duties involved with young children. He did not smoke, only drank socially and never raised his voice or got into arguments. The downside was his wandering ways of course and he was very much inclined to keep things to himself. Consequently I always felt there was a distance between us. Crucially I knew I did not love him, although he said he loved me but I suppose I married him for practical reasons. I was living in a small town, everyone knew each other's business, I had two children and needed stability in my life and he provided it. Thus we decided to get married and applied for a licence which took three months to come through. The wedding was attended by about fifteen people including my relations (by this time my mother was living with another man) and his family from Lubana. About a month after the wedding we received a letter from his mother's sister who lived somewhere in Russia announcing she was coming to see us. She stayed about a week and was a quiet woman who caused no trouble during her time with us. After she got back home she must have spoken to her sister, Pavel's mother, because a few weeks later she too came to see us from far off Siberia. She came laden down with gifts, including lots of good quality warm clothing for me and masses of food such as a giant salted salmon and a bucket of pine nuts. She was very friendly and pleasant on arrival but she had obviously not been told I had two children because when she shortly found out her attitude seemed to change and there was a definite coolness in her behaviour.

Nevertheless, we had conversations about the possibility of us moving to their area of Siberia, which was a city called Dalnegorsk some 500 kilometres from Vladivostok and I was quite receptive to the idea. Vladimir was still making a nuisance of himself as I had to see him from time to time when handing over the children or bringing them back, apart from bumping into him in the town whether by his design or by accident and in addition the small town atmosphere was becoming increasingly oppressive to me. Although the move meant relocating to a place about ten thousand kilometres distant, of which I knew nothing, I ended up thinking 'why not?' and we started making plans for the move. Our furniture would have to be shipped by sea in a container so this involved us having to travel to another Latvian town, Gulbene, to make the arrangements. After a couple of weeks hearing nothing, it was decided that Pavel would go back there and find out what was the cause of the delay. He went on his own and was gone three days without word. When he returned I was unable to find out what had happened and to this day I never knew for certain, but I can only guess that it involved him coming to some arrangement with a woman there. He came back with loads of presents at a time when there were shortages of sweets and confectionery and my suspicions were obviously aroused, but the container was available and we booked our flight. We were now committed to going and we made a very satisfactory arrangement with the local authority about our flat, which would remain in our name but be sublet to other tenants in our absence. We took a flight from Riga to Khabakovsk in a large Tupelev aircraft and had to change there for the flight to Vladivostok, which was a further 750 kilometres. Once there, we were now wanting to get to our ultimate destination but there were no more airplane flights available that day and we ended up completing the journey to Dalnegorsk, which as I have said, was about 500 kilometres, by helicopter. This was a horrible experience for me, the ride was frightening as the helicopter seemed to be forever headed straight into a mountain or climbing vertically the next minute with my heart in my mouth. I was very sick as a result of it but we finally got there after a long, long journey to our new home near the Sea of

Japan, a world away from Madona. It was spring 1984.

Pavel's parents lived in a rural setting a few miles from the city in a three bed house with a huge barn where they stored the food for their animals. They kept a bull, cows, pigs, chickens and geese. They had a large apple orchard and grew vegetables as well. The house had a large cold room full of provisions for the winter. We stayed with them until our container finally arrived in the port and we were able to go to the city and look for accommodation and work. Surrounded by the beautiful mountainous countryside, Dalnegorsk itself was an industrial city with a large number of brickworks, chemical industries and factories that were on permanent standby to be converted to munitions works at 24 hours notice. The air was polluted and children were often born with genetic defects ranging from heart problems to brain damage. Of course, this was all unknown to me before we moved there. By way of compensation, the shops were full of good food, particularly fresh fish – crab, calamari, white fish etc – and the clothes shops had the latest fashions, imported from Japan, which was of course the other side of the sea.

Pavel got a job in one of the factories but my opportunities were limited because of my two young children so I took a job at a kindergarten which they also attended. One of his friends put us in touch with a divorced man who had a three bed flat and we rented one room in the flat, sharing the kitchen and toilet. This man was an alcoholic who regularly stole our food although I frequently offered him what I had cooked anyway. From my window I could see the nearby mountains and often wondered why they seemed to be pink. I found out the answer one day when Pavel returned with an armful of wild peonies which he had picked from the mountainside, and a large amount of pink rosemary flowers. He had apparently been challenged on the bus as to why he had picked wild flowers which was against the law, but on saying they were for his wife, nothing further was said.

That said, Pavel was turning out to be a somewhat different character in his own country. He was no longer so quiet and unargumentative and we had frequent fallings-out. History was also about to repeat itself. One evening, a woman I worked with at the kindergarten came round for a few drinks and we had a pleasant evening with Pavel singing and playing his guitar. When the time came for her to go home, we offered to walk back with her. I suddenly had a strange presentiment about this, and made an excuse to go to the toilet while they started the walk back to her place, me following at a distance where I could not be seen. On reaching their destination, they went inside and left the curtains open and a window was slightly ajar, so I came up close and could hear them talking. I walked home and went to bed and it was about three of four hours before Pavel returned home, went to sleep and nothing was said. All he had to say the next morning was that he had stayed there for a couple of drinks before coming home and I never raised the subject again.

We moved to a house which had a big kitchen and living room and a nice garden full of apple trees and vegetables which the owner, who lived some distance away, looked after. My mother in law presented us with a piglet, which I grew very attached to and did not like the idea of us eventually eating. She grew very large in the coming months and with winter coming on I noticed she had large swelling which a neighbour told me was fatal. On her word, Pavel had my pig slaughtered while I was at work, which made me very sad as I was very fond of her. What made it worse was that we heard afterwards that my neighbour had been mistaken and my sow was simply keen on finding a mate.

My mother in law bought Pavel a car which cost around 8000 Roubles and we had an invitation to have a meal with our landlord in recognition that we were good tenants and were looking after his property well. He lived about a half hour's drive across the city, so we went by car. We had a very nice meal during which we drank moderately but I was not sure exactly what we were drinking and soon became aware that I was getting drunk. Pavel was also in the same condition and when we started to drive home it was really no surprise that we were stopped by the police. As the driver, he was arrested and was to be taken to the police station where he would spend a night in the cells. This left me stranded, a long way from home and with no money to pay for a taxi home, even if I could find one. Unfortunately, displaying that volatile temperament I had, as I have said before, inherited from my grandmother, and worsened by drink, I started shouting and raging at the police officer, using language even I was not aware I knew. I remember I also threatened him that if I had a Kalashnikov handy, he would know about it. The result was I also spent the night in a cell which I had to share with two other women. I tried to distance myself from them and slept on the floor near the door. Every so often, a guard would open the small window and ask if I was alright and offered me water, which I was glad to accept. In the morning during my court appearance I was told that my situation would have to be reported to my employer, which might cost me my job, but I was let off with a warning as to my future behaviour. As for Pavel, he had already been dealt with and had driven off in the car without waiting to find out what had happened to me. I was taken home by an officer and fortunately, although no one was home, a window was slightly open and I was able to climb in. At work, I was hauled in before a panel and given a severe verbal reprimand, but not sacked so it could have been worse. Pavel was gone for about three days and I never found out, nor asked, what he had been doing.

There were many good things about the house we lived in, but as winter came on we found it was very cold and after a snowfall, very difficult to even open the front door to get out. Inside, the windows were thick with frost and there was no adequate heating. The local authority found us another flat, this time we had one room and had to share kitchen and toilet with the other tenants. The people with whom we shared the flat had a young son who was under a year old but who was very disturbed, crying a lot during the night and keeping us awake, but at least it was warm and much healthier for the children. .

I was now pregnant again and this time, unlike previously, I was actually looking forward to my new baby, which my mother in law wrongly predicted would be a boy and I felt happy about my pregnancy and life in general and Christmas was close. At my place of work they were organising a big party with plenty of food and drink but we decided to stay at home and have a quiet

Christmas on our own. However, as the evening wore on and the children were asleep in bed, as it was only about ten minutes away from our flat, we decided to join the party after all and turned up with some food and drink and sat down with the rest of crowd. During the evening I noticed one woman staring at Pavel for quite some time and after a while she got up and left the room, presumably to go to the ladies room. After about ten minutes Pavel also got up to go to the toilet which made me suspicious in view of previous experience. I then decided to find out what was going on and started to search the building. The party was being held upstairs, so I went to the ground floor where I heard sounds coming from the basement. Going towards the stairs, I saw two people emerging, hurriedly adjusting their clothing. I saw a red mist, and picking up with both hands a coffee table that was nearby, hurled it at them as forcefully as I could and quickly left for home. Once again, Pavel never explained the incident and we did not speak about it again, but shortly I was hauled in before my employer's again because the woman had had the audacity to write a letter of complaint about my behaviour, causing her bruising etc. The outcome was that I was given a written warning about my future conduct and was told that next time anything similar happened, I would be sacked. The fact that my feelings about my husband's infidelity and her part in it were not taken into account left me with a burning sense of injustice. The feeling of unfairness in how the matter was handled was a corrosive force in my head and I have from then on never felt any faith or confidence in the ability of courts, panels or any kind of judicial body to deliver real justice to the accused person and I am sorry to say, that as a Latvian person in a predominantly Russian region, I felt this was a factor as well.

In my in-laws' village, we were invited to a neighbour's birthday party and turning up at the door, I was somehow propelled to the front and was thus the first person to enter the house. An old lady who I did not know greeted me warmly, took my hand and welcomed me, telling me how beautiful I was, that she had seen me from a distance before but that now close up, I was even finer than she had thought, a princess etc. She went on to tell Pavel that he did not deserve me and I was far above him, which made me feel good but no doubt did not please him! During the evening, he drank too much and went to sleep in his chair, and I remember wiping the slobber from his mouth and cleaning his nose. He had to be helped the short distance home as he was unable to stand up by himself.

The following day we went back to the flat and found that our co-tenants were moving to be near their parents in another area where their son could get better attention, and we were able to take over the whole of the flat, which greatly improved things as far as our accommodation was concerned.

Pavel's friends at work invited him on a fishing trip so I was told which would involve him going to the Sea of Japan in an area which was within reach of Dalnegorsk but would involve being away from home for a few days. I pointed out to him that he had no fishing gear, either clothes or equipment but was told that his friends had enough to sort him out. They turned up for him at 6 am one morning and he was gone about three days. When he came back it was without any fish.

CHAPTER 5

My daughter Olga was born on July 24, 1985 and we came home together from the hospital. Perhaps it was because I was a more experienced mother now, perhaps it was because I felt such love for her, but she was a very contented baby, never cried and slept well. She had beautiful black hair, brown eyes like her father and paternal grandmother and long eyelashes. I loved to hold her in my arms and gently rub her nose, tickle her and see her mouth open in a toothless, gummy smile. I got into a routine of seeing to the next day's baby food at night after the children were asleep. Sterilising the bottles, using buckwheat, oats and milk blended into a porridge and then decanted into baby bottles ready for the next day. The milk came from the cows on my in-laws' smallholding, brought by my father in law once a week. These were the days before disposable nappies and we had no washing machine so I had to scrub the cotton nappies clean on my washboard, soak them in the bath and dry them before getting to bed about 1 o'clock in the morning. After a few weeks I developed excruciating pains in my stomach. I went to the doctor, who sent me home, simply advising me to get some rest but the pains got worse and I was finally admitted to hospital. It turned out I had an ectopic pregnancy and I was operated on immediately. This was in the days before laser surgery and I was rather brutally sliced open in the process and of course still bear the scar to this day. Very weak, I could hardly move and faced a long period of recovery in hospital. One day I was told I had a visitor but being under quarantine, I would have to get dressed and go out to the corridor to meet Pavel, who was carrying Olga in his arms. The local climate was subject to extremes – sweltering hot in the summer but an early winter with temperatures soon plunging to double digit minuses - so by early October the snow had arrived and it was freezing cold outside. Our baby was not suitably clothed for the weather and it was no surprise to find that she soon developed pneumonia. The childrens' hospital was adjacent to the one I was in and she was taken there for treatment. I learned that Pavel was there with her and in my weakened state I decided to try to walk the short distance to see them. What should have been a couple of minutes or so took me ages as I was so lacking in strength I could hardly walk and it was about -50c below outside. There was no help forthcoming to escort me of course – a lack of common humanity was sadly a characteristic of the bureaucratic structure of Soviet society and not much has changed in the intervening years. However, on reaching the children's hospital I was shocked to see how ill my daughter was. The doctor in charge was at pains to tell me how good Pavel had been in caring for her and that she could not have been in better hands but I could see she was desperately ill, with her nose blocked up so that breathing was very difficult. She was obviously too young to know how to blow her nose and Pavel on several occasions managed to clear the blockage by sucking the accumulated mucous from her nose with his mouth, which was a truly admirable thing to do.

I was allowed home after a couple of weeks while Pavel and Olga had to remain in hospital for two weeks more while she recovered from pneumonia and my two other children were with Pavel's parents while I recuperated.

When Olga came home I realised how much I had missed her and was very glad to be reunited with her. We saw however, that her ears were quite noticeably sticking out, and when she was sleeping they would be completely doubled up whichever side she slept on. The system back then was that a doctor would visit recently born babies once a month to check that all was well and we discussed this with him. He suggested that she wear a tight cotton bonnet at night to keep her ears flat to her head so that they could not fold over but when we checked at night, that is exactly what happened. This was a problem that was only rectified by an operation many years later. Other than that, she soon developed into a chubby, smiley little girl who began to crawl after a few months and started walking at about nine months.

Meanwhile Liana and Sergei went to the kindergarten and I was on maternity leave, which was for a very generous three years. For the first year, I received around 50% of my wages, reducing thereafter. The old Soviet system had many good points, as well as the obvious disadvantages. I got into the habit of going out with Olga in her pram, and found a spot by a syringa bush where there was a bench and soon became friendly with a young woman named Anna who lived in the same block of flats, on the fourth floor. She was married with two daughters aged about 10 and 4, her husband was in prison having killed someone but was due for release in a couple of years or so. Although he had been in prison for some time, conjugal visits were allowed, the four year old being the fruit of one such visit. Anna was to play a part in later events as I will relate.

I found out that there was a cleaning job at a school quite nearby, about a ten or fifteen minute walk, so I started working in the evenings which took about two hours. I had a whole floor to clean with an endless corridor off which there were about ten classrooms. This was fine in the summer, but as winter came on it was dangerous to walk out at night as wild animals from the mountains were known to venture into the outskirts of the city where we lived and the idea of being faced with bears and even tigers on the way to and from work was not an inviting prospect. I tried working early mornings instead but as the school opened at about eight o'clock this meant a very early start. After about three months I had had enough.

One day Pavel suggested a fishing trip but this time taking me and Olga. I went along with the idea and I packed some provisions, warm clothing and a tent in the car. Strangely, we set off fairly late in the day to head for the beach and the Sea of Japan but as usual I suspected nothing. We arrived at our destination and it was extremely windy, not conditions suitable for what was planned. Pavel got out of the car telling me he was going to speak with a friend and headed for a nearby block of flats. He was gone for about one hour and when he got back it was only to tell me that we were going home, without any further explanation.

One day I was at my usual place on the bench with Olga in her pram when two of his work colleagues appeared. They were the men he had supposedly been fishing with on that unsuccessful trip I mentioned earlier. They had come to tell me something which perhaps I should have known all along. First though it was about work. They had sent Pavel to Coventry, as the English expression is. The reason was that at their works, they had a room where they changed into their work clothes, leaving their normal clothes on pegs. The men had noticed that money left in their pockets had gone missing and they set out to find the thief. Pavel was caught redhanded helping himself to money from someone's pocket. As he had a wife and family it was decided not to report him to management but from then on no one would speak to him or associate with him. This was a bad enough revelation, but what they had to say about the fishing trip was even worse. Apparently the weather was too bad to go out fishing so they spent the time in the flat, obviously the same one that Pavel had gone to when I was with him. Pavel had spent three nights with this woman and although I had strongly suspected something like this, it was another thing to be told that this was actually what had happened.

When he came home that evening, I confronted him with what I had been told. I was no longer interested in explanations, I had been given proof of his unfaithfulness and from now on he could go his way and I would go mine. I slept in the childrens' room and left him to it and he started to drink with the usual results of slobber and dribble.

The next day was going to be the start of a new life and I went to a nearby dressmaker and ordered an expensive dress made of the best material and embroidered with flowers which was paid for by the last of my kindergarten money. When it was ready, I dressed up and went with a couple of my friends into the city and we went to an expensive restaurant and night club where we had a lovely meal, some drinks and danced. One man asked me to dance and we did so several times but the last bus home was at 11.30 so we left together. His name was Alexander, which brought back memories of another with the same name, and he was very pleasant to talk to. However, with all the drink, I had to answer a call of nature by jumping off the bus and he followed me.   After this embarrassment by the roadside, he walked me home. He suggested we meet again and I said 'maybe' and went to my front door. As I quietly opened it, Pavel suddenly appeared, slapped me violently in the face with such force that I fell backwards down a small flight of maybe six or seven steps and landed on my back on the hard concrete floor. I took a long time to get to sleep as my back was hurting really badly but on reflection I suppose I was lucky it was not my head.   This incident made up my minds that a divorce was the only way out of this.

Pavel had problems with an ear dating back to childhood and when he consulted a doctor was told that a bone was badly decayed and he would need to go to a hospital in Vladivostok for an operation as his condition was potentially life threatening. Before he went he was full of contrition, saying how sorry he was for all the pain he had caused me and that things would be different if we could try again when he came back from hospital. We did not have a telephone at home but there was a bureau in the city where calls could be made and so we kept in touch that way. One day, the hospital could not find him when I rang but after a long delay I was told they had eventually found him in the grounds smoking. I decided to go to Vladivostok to see him. This was a long train journey but eventually I arrived at the hospital. Again, he was nowhere to be found and it was only when I spoke to a cleaner that I was told where he was. This was upstairs from his own level and I went up to the room she had told me, quietly opened the door and found him having sex with a woman on her bed.

Two days later he came home, pleading again on his hands and knees that he had been in hospital for a month and needed sex and this woman meant nothing to him, in fact she was repulsive etc etc. By now I was working out how I could manage to get back to Latvia and leave all this behind me, so I would save as much money as I could from the weekly necessities. About this time I was on the receiving end of an injured wife's anger, but this was entirely innocent. A colleague from work had invited me to go round to her flat for a social evening and we had a few drinks with her neighbour, whose wife had gone away on a visit for a couple of days. When we ran out of supplies, he invited me upstairs to help myself from his well stocked bar to whatever drink I liked and take it back down to my friend's flat. Nothing happened, it was all very civilised and I thought no more about it. A few days later, there was a rapid knock on my door and this lady asked to come in as there was something she wished to discuss with me. It turned out that she was the neighbour's wife and my so called friend had told her about my innocent visit to her flat. I was able to straighten her out without any ceremony.

At weekends that year between July and August we used to go to his parents house in the village and go with them by car into the mountainous forests to pick wild blueberries, The drive itself was quite hair raising with narrow mountain roads, many dangerous bends and no safety barriers of course, but once we got to the forests the results were rewarding. Huge Siberian blueberries grew on bushes as tall as I was and we spent all day picking them, filling up the car boot with bucketloads of these tasty berries. I had been used to picking blueberries in the forests around Madona, but these were in a different category, in both size and flavour. Returning to the village, my mother in law kept what she needed to make jams and compotes but the rest Pavel took to a market in the city and was able to sell a bucket of maybe 10 litres of berries for 15 roubles, and we had many buckets.

With winter approaching and little Olga not in the best of health following her bout of pneumonia, it was necessary to get her some warm clothes for the winter and there was a woman in a nearby flat who was an expert knitter. I got her to knit some beautiful warm clothes for Olga, jumpers, cardigans, leggings and a fleece lined bonnet, in lovely bright colours. This was paid for with the proceeds of our berry picking. When she had finished making them we left them with Pavel's parents to look after until such time as they were needed.

CHAPTER 6

One day I was again in my usual position on the bench and was thinking about recent events and crying, when a man came up to me and started talking. He had been divorced about six months ago but his ex wife still shared his flat and they had a 14 year old son. The man's name was Alexander, which I could hardly believe in view of my previous friendship with a man of the same name, and we quickly struck up a warm relationship, going for walks and spending time talking to each other. One day he invited me to come to his flat for a drink but his son took exception to my presence and I left. There was a woman I knew who had a flat where she was prepared to let us have one room so we decided to take it and I remember it took only two suitcases for me to pack, one for me and one for the children. When Pavel came home, I was gone.

Of course in those days we had no telephone so I wrote to my mother in law asking her to send the clothes that I had had knitted for Olga to my new address. She replied that as I had treated her son so badly she was not going to send them. I replied that it her granddaughter's wellbeing we were concerned with, not the rights and wrongs of my relationship with her son, and that if she had any regard for her Olga, she should send them without any delay. She replied that she could not, as she had sat down one evening by her kitchen stove and had burnt them all, one by one.

The people with whom we shared the flat could not have been nicer and despite the cramped conditions we never had a cross word, although things like sharing the kitchen were not easy. It was only a temporary situation in any case and I was very happy with Alexander, who was an ideal partner, kind and considerate and I truly loved him. For the first time in my life I knew what real love was, I was all dewy eyed and my head used to go dizzy when I was near him. He was wonderful with the children. My daughter Olga in particular used to be always in his arms, and I remember one time he was playing with her holding her above him when she suddenly felt the need to pass water full in his face and he never reacted at all. His ex wife used to keep calling on us with some pretext or other needing his help and he kept forestalling her until one day his son called saying his mother was very ill and would he go to see her. Although they had been divorced for some time she was still hopeful of getting him back but he made it clear to her that would not happen.
We started to plan our future together and decided it would be best to go to Latvia and start a new life there. He was a highly qualified mechanic and engineer and had a very good job involving operating heavy duty bulldozers on construction

sites so finding work should not be a problem and of course we had the flat to go back to in Madona. He gave notice at his job and was working out the two weeks notice required and we started making preparations for the move. I had left a few belongings at my old flat with Pavel and went back there one day to collect them. To my surprise my key did not turn the lock and after about five minutes of door knocking, Pavel opened the door and behind him was my friend Anna, both of them by the look of it having hurriedly re-dressed. She was at pains to tell me that this had only started after I had left, but I still felt betrayed by someone I had counted on as a friend.

Alexander had to go to his works to collect some paperwork and I went with him, waiting in an office while he went about his business. After a while, I decided to go outside and as I did so, his wife appeared holding a large stone above her head which she was about to hurl at me when Alexander rushed up behind her and grabbed it before she could throw it.

We arranged to stay at a hotel for three nights before our departure. I telegrammed my mother to say we were coming home and that I was not alone! The journey involved a plane to Vladivostok and then a direct flight to Riga, and of course infinitely preferable to a week long train journey, which was the other alternative. However, we had to stay in Vladivostok overnight and this was when a fateful decision was made which would have the most unhappy consequences. It was a fact that working in the extreme weather conditions that prevailed in that part of the Soviet Union was very rewarding in terms of salaries and wages which far exceeded those available in other regions. Alexander had mentioned the prospects of working in Yakutsk, a city in the north where the weather was extreme but where pay for his kind of work was likely to be very high. We talked about this during the evening and it was decided that he would go there and seek work and accommodation and then send for me in a short time. This seemed to make sense although I did not like the idea of being separated so soon. I remember him on the waving off terrace as I sat on the plane with the children, watching him becoming a speck in the distance and wondering when I would see him again.

CHAPTER 7

When I arrived back in Madona I had trouble with the tenants who were living in my flat. They refused to leave and I had to go to court to get a judgement against them. Fortunately, the magistrate found in my favour and they were evicted so we were all set to live there. While this was happening, I was receiving letters from Alexander, who confessed that he thought we had made a big mistake and he should have come with me. He was working deep in the forests around the city where his accommodation was shared with only other men, in a primitive log cabin lacking essential services and obviously not fit for me to join him. Perhaps after six months he would come to Latvia. By this time, I discovered I was pregnant and felt in a hopeless situation. Three children, one more on the way, no money, no job, not a stick of furniture, so I made a fateful decision. The baby was aborted and I wrote and told him that it was over and would he please send me my possessions (he had taken all the luggage when we left to Yakutsk). No more letters were sent or received and eventually my suitcases turned up. I have made many wrong decisions in my life and many mistakes too but this was by far the biggest and most costly for my future happiness. There are moments in life when although you have no tears in your eyes, in your heart is a full ocean of tears, so full you feel your heart will explode. I hope no one will judge me because only I know how I felt. The one thing in life that is worth fighting for is your family, but I missed my chance.

Soon after my return to Madona, I wrote to Pavel and told him I was seeking a divorce and sent the necessary application to the authorities. In my letter I took the opportunity to set the record straight over matters about which I had kept my silence over the years. I set out the numerous times he had been unfaithful to me going back to our early times together in Madona and how much he had hurt me by his actions and finished by writing about his mother's burning of his daughter's clothes. I said how much I regretted moving to Dalnegorsk and wondered if things would have been different if we had stayed in Latvia, but somehow I doubt it. My letter was never answered.

I had to make arrangements about some insurance policy, the details of which I cannot remember but I called at the office to see a woman named Astride, who was my neighbour and who worked there. Whilst waiting in the corridor a woman came out of another office and as she approached me I recognised her as a cousin of Pavel's who I had met some while ago when we were living in Madona previously. What she told me was a complete shock – did I know that Pavel was dead? I broke down and cried. Although we were no longer together, he was still a young man and a tragedy that he had died. I tried to make arrangements to fly back for his funeral and went to Riga airport to try to buy a ticket, which would have involved flying to Moscow, changing planes to fly to Vladivostok and changing again to get to Dalnegorsk. However, it was just my luck that it was the time of year when the Supreme Soviet Party congress was taking place in Moscow that week and all flights via Moscow were out of the question. There was no other way of getting there in time and the funeral could not be postponed. I very much wanted to be there to say goodbye but regrettably, there was nothing I could do.

Later, I was able speak to a former neighbour in that block of flats where we had lived with Pavel, to find out exactly what had happened. She told me that after I had left him, he was drunk most of the time. He had also taken up with Anna, who you may recall I had previously thought of as my friend, and who lived on the fourth floor. I mentioned earlier that her husband was serving a prison sentence for murder but was due for release at some indeterminate time in the near future. What happened next is not clear, but apparently Pavel had been in Anna's flat when her husband suddenly turned up without warning, having just been released from prison. The next morning Pavel was found dead on the ground immediately beneath the balcony, presumably having fallen to his death. The exact circumstances were never established, although speculation was rife. Whether there had been a confrontation between the two men or perhaps he had been trying to escape via the balcony to avoid trouble is unknown and I was never aware of any legal action that might have been taken later. The death certificate stated cause of death as subdural haematoma which was hardly surprising in view of the fall from such a height, but unexplained events always lead you to wonder what really happened. Subsequently, I learned that my mother in law died a year or so later from cancer and that chapter in my life came to a close.

CHAPTER 8

I had made up my mind that from now on, there would be no more permanent relationships with men after my experiences. I would please myself who I saw, would occasionally meet a man for casual social and possibly sexual pleasure, but never anything serious or regular. I always took care never to take anyone home for my children to see, it was always at the man's flat or house and was entirely self-contained. I was finally in control of my life after years of subservience to my parents and abusive men, or so I thought at the time.

I found employment at a kindergarten in Madona where my children could be accommodated as well but it was to last only four days. One day in the town I bumped into my uncle, the one who had years before tipped me off about Vladimir's infidelity. He was on his way to a doctor's appointment and had lots of shopping with him which he asked me to take home to my place and he would collect later. Also included was a magazine which I put into my bag. I should mention that my uncle was a very talented artist who had attended art school and later found employment in the fledgling but up and coming Latvian film industry as a set decorator and designer. His flat was crammed full of books and magazines, which were his passion, together with his work but he was somewhat absent minded and did not collect his things that night. I went to work at the kindergarten the next day and during the course of the morning, my boss who was processing my job details, asked for my passport as part of her checks. I promptly opened my bag to retrieve it, taking out my uncle's magazine which was the topmost of the bag's contents and to my horror and that of my boss, the magazine's cover displayed a nude woman. I looked at her and she looked at me and she promptly left the room. Within a few minutes, her superior came into the room and told me in icy tones that my services were no longer required and that my children were not welcome either. I could offer no explanation as I was completely taken by surprise and had no idea that the magazine was pornographic, something that was banned in Latvia at the time.

In a state of shock, I returned home and when my uncle called later that day there was of course a lively exchange of views about the consequences of his actions, causing me to lose my job after only four days in such embarrassing circumstances. I now had to find new employment and a woman who had been a witness at my first wedding pointed me in the right direction. There was a vacancy at the local authority department in charge of sanitary inspections of businesses; nowadays I suppose it has the title of Environmental Health or some such grand title. The job was not well paid but I found it very enjoyable and all the staff got on well together. My function was to inspect premises to make sure they were adhering to the standards of the time and was mainly concerned with cockroaches, rats and mice. Unlike my time at the mink farm, this time I was provided with protective equipment and a driver who ferried the team from place to place. We were kept very busy with a regular programme of disinfestation and disinfection at cafes, restaurants, shops, factories and the whole range of businesses. Although Latvia was still in the Soviet Union at this time in the late 1980s, the authorities in Riga were already starting to carry out a programme of Latvianisation of government departments and one day an edict went out that all reports we made had to be in Latvian. Most of my colleagues were only Russian speaking and I was the only one with bilingual abilities so I ended up being burdened with having to write all their reports as well as finding time for my own work. However, as I have said, generally we had a good time, with meetings every morning to discuss the day's events where there were ample refreshments and a relaxed atmosphere.

After I had been in the job a few months I received a letter from the local housing authority that the building I was living in, which as I have said was an old wooden barn, was being demolished and that I would be placed in temporary housing while a new purpose built five storey block of flats was being built on the site. This was planned to take about a year. The new accommodation was a somewhat unusual set up as I was allocated two adjacent flats on the same corridor. Both had one room and a kitchen so I had Olga with me in one and the other was for Liana and Sergei. There was an outside shed for wood and the toilet facilities were communal. I had a large tub to bath the children with water from pans heated on the wood stove as there was only a cold water tap. For a proper adult bath you had to go to the municipal baths and sauna for which of course you had to pay.

About this time I would occasionally have a social visit from a woman who knew my mother. She worked as a cook at the local hospital and had a disconcerting astigmatism which meant you could never tell if she was looking at you or indeed speaking to you if more than one person was present. She was not really a friend of mine, but she would come for a coffee or sometimes we would have a drink of cognac. One day she brought this man with her who she had a kind of relationship with. I thought nothing more of it. Janis was his name and he was well known as a lazy good for nothing who seldom kept a job and would sponge off any woman who would feed and clothe him.

A few days later he turned up at my flat without invitation and although I made it clear I was not interested in any close relationship we would see each other occasionally on a purely social basis. One evening, I had a small gathering at my flat when the drinks were flowing and I obviously had too much because when I woke up the next morning, to my horror I sensed someone was beside me in the bed. I had no memory of what had happened but there was Janis. I never could remember what had happened but when I discovered I was pregnant again my worst fears were realised. It was as if history was repeating itself but I had no intention of going ahead with the pregnancy nor of having a close relationship with this man. However, it was impossible to find a doctor who would abort the baby despite me travelling all around the region to try to find someone.

I therefore had to go ahead with the pregnancy and continued to see Janis from time to time. My daughter Vita was born on 12th October 1986. Janis was only mildly interested in her so it was not difficult to finally stop seeing him and try to bring up my new baby and my other three children as best I could. I still had my job of course and fortunately was able to develop another profitable sideline which made the world of difference to my fortunes.

There was a woman named Valentina who I had been friendly with at school although she was a year ahead of me. We used to go to discos together in my teenage years but over the years we had lost touch and she had married a man from Ukraine. One day I happened to meet her in the town and she invited me back to her place for a coffee. I found out that she made her own vodka and she showed me what was necessary to produce it. She assured me it was very easy to make so I asked her to come to my flat and show me how it was done. This she did and I started up my own production without difficulty. One of my neighbours happened to know one of the men who was involved in building the new block of flats and when she saw the results of my labours and had sampled them she offered to try to sell it to the men on the building site. My vodka was an immediate success and I was soon producing about 10 litres a week, which paid so well I soon had a large tin full of money which I didn't even bother to count. This was of course an illegal activity but the authorities if they knew, turned a blind eye to it. I suspect the reason was that although I was entitled to social security, I never claimed it and I have reason to believe that someone in the office siphoned it off for themselves, so the one cancelled out the other.

By now the new flat was ready and I went with Vita in her pushchair to see our new home, a three bedroom flat on the second floor. It was in a fairly dirty state and the floors and walls needed a lot of cleaning which took about a week. The heating system was provided by the local authority and would not be available until October 1, a few weeks hence so it was very cold to start with. Gas was not available yet so I bought a small electric cooker and we had a sofa to sleep on. Olga was with my mother and Liana and Sergei stayed with Vladimir's mother while the flat was being readied. I was able to get some basic furniture for the childrens' rooms and some good quality curtains but there was a serious shortage of larger items such as wardrobes and fitted units. I had negotiations with the furniture store and ended up going to lunch with the owner after which I gave him a list of all the things that were necessary. One of the luxuries in the new flat was a telephone line and I bought a beautiful telephone, the first I had ever owned. One day it rang and I was told to get down to the store where I found myself one of the first in the queue which had started to form. Unbelievably, I queued for three days and nights waiting for my furniture to arrive, during which time I was relieved in the queue by various family members who took it in turns. Such shortages were commonplace in Latvia at that time, hard as it is to believe that now. Notwithstanding, I was very happy to be the proud owner of some lovely furniture, including a fitted wall to wall storage unit consisting of wardrobes and ample cupboard space above. All paid for by the proceeds of my illegal bootleg vodka.

I was happy that following my break up with Alexander, I had made a new life for myself and I found I had renewed energy and purpose to my existence that would have been unthinkable a few years before. One of the results of this was that I started another source of income. I was continuing my successful vodka operation but a fresh opportunity arose. This was in 1987 before Poland gained independence from the Soviet Union, although there was a lot of agitation and unrest in the country. However, I found out that there was a regular coach service that went to Poland that was mainly comprised of Latvians bringing all kinds of consumer goods to sell in Polish markets. It could be food, electrical appliances, small household gadgets, anything that could be transported easily and having been bought at cheap prices locally, could be sold for a tidy profit in Poland, where everything was very expensive. It would take a day to get there and one day to return, but you had three days in between to sell these goods at local markets. Firstly, I had to try to arrange this at work to have time off to do this. My boss was very supportive, in return for supplying her with some consumer items, she covered for me at work and once a month I was able to make the trip without losing any of my regular income.

We would go to various cities – Warsaw, Gdansk, Katowice for example - and this carried on for some time. I was able to obtain food from my aunt's shop under the rationing scheme that still applied in Latvia and this was also an opportunity to sell my home brewed vodka. I also had many acquaintances in shops in the town where I could obtain goods under the counter so stock was never a problem. The coach trips were not very comfortable but as soon as we started the journey, people would begin drinking, including the driver sometimes, and the atmosphere was good. The problems arose when it came to toilet stops, quite frequent because of the amount of drink consumed. There were no motorway stations with proper facilities on the journey, so I am sorry to say that we were forced to stop by the roadside and disappear en masse into a nearby forest. Sometimes, depending where we were based in Poland, we were able to stay at a nunnery where they had dormitories where we could be accommodated, arranged by the courier and free of charge. We were also able to use their bathroom and toilet facilities for which we were very grateful. The nuns were very kind to us and we left them with gifts in return. They had a gift shop and I bought an icon of Jesus in a beautiful frame which shone in the dark at night and which I still have. Other times we were not so lucky and had to sleep on the coach and go without a proper wash all week.

The border controls were quite lax but occasionally we would be warned that a more rigorous check would take place. I soon learned to hide my vodka supplies in the long sleeves of my large overcoat, in inside pockets and all sorts of other places, including adapting thermos flasks as improvised vodka bottles. The derivation of 'bootleg' was also something I learned from first hand experience as I used my long winter boots for their obvious purpose as well.

Many people came home with just the money they had raised but I always took the opportunity to look out for good clothes for my children and myself, and bring them home some tasty treats that we could not get in Latvia. Back home, my eldest, Liana was a very responsible girl of about twelve by now and I used to leave her in charge of the children, supplemented by regular visits from my mother to make sure all was well. Liana kept the flat beautifully clean and was a good cook. I would get home late at night from one of these journeys and all would be silent, until she heard me moving around and woke up the others, whereupon I would give them a few treats I had brought home with me. I was pleased and proud that my children were well dressed, even compared to regular families where the man was the breadwinner but one of Liana's teachers was very critical of the fact that she was wearing such good clothes to school and admonished her for it.

As I have said, this new life of mine left no time nor inclination for personal relationships but inevitably I got drawn into one. There was a man on the coach who although from Riga had dropped off in Madona to visit his wife's family and he started to pay me attention. We got to talking and as there was an empty seat next to mine at the back of the coach, asked if he could sit next to me. On subsequent trips, this became a habit and if he was first on the coach, used to save a seat for me. In between he would write to me or phone and we eventually slept together.

I have mentioned the drinking on the coach but I had a low tolerance to alcohol and decided to stop drinking. On one particular journey, he sat as usual sat next to me and I noticed a woman nearby, whom I knew as someone of very loose morals, kept giving him the eye. He was keen to drink and I wasn't, so he asked if I minded if he sat with her. I told him he was free to do as he wished and he spent the rest of the journey with her. On our frequent stops I felt very embarrassed as the whole coach knew about what had happened. Needless to say, some people took delight in pointing it out to me. After a couple of weeks, and having had no contact with him, there was a knock on my door and he stood outside. This man, who had a wife and children, had apparently contracted venereal disease from this woman and was in big trouble with his wife as a result. I showed him the door and was thankful that I had finished with him, but it was yet another episode that taught me one more lesson.

CHAPTER 9

I was as a settled now as at any time in my life. I had a steady, if not very remunerative job, I had a couple of sidelines to supplement my income and we were living in reasonable accommodation. I had no man in my life to cause me any problems and my children were well fed and dressed. Vladimir was paying me alimony but was now not causing me any problems and Janis only very occasionally appeared on the scene. On one such occasion I was able to turn this to my advantage as well. He telephoned me to say that he had been working for about a month on a well paid job but was shortly to leave and was going to be away from Madona for a while on a new job. This necessitated him acquiring a new wardrobe of clothes and footwear and it just so happened that I had a fair amount of gear that I had bought in Poland and was looking to sell, which worked out well for both of us. As I have said, he was never much interested in the welfare of his daughter but after we had concluded our business transaction he produced a box of chocolate liqueurs filled with vodka as a present for her.   Its inappropriateness for a young child never occurred to him, which pretty much summed him up!

My Polish import/export business was going well as was the home made vodka and I was also able to develop an extra source of income from my regular job. The disinfestation and disinfectant products of which I had access to at work were much in demand outside the official dispensation of the sanitation department. Every day I would requisition the required quantities for distribution that day but as I was in control of them I was always able to keep some back for my private clients, particularly in the local villages where I was well known for selling my other wares. These private sales were far more profitable than my regular income from the job.

However, in life, things never stand still for long, the river runs on but beneath the surface there are imperceptible eddies and undercurrents which eventually cause a change of direction. So it was to happen shortly, but it was in part brought about by a family tragedy that caused a great amount of grief and regret.

I have spoken of my aunt Marija, who was my father's sister and who worked in a food shop. She had been an army careerist in her younger days and while on duty in Kazakhstan, had married a young man from Almaty. They had two children, a daughter and a son but my grandmother was against the marriage and probably instrumental in them breaking up and getting divorced. Marija never remarried and lived with her mother and the two children in Madona. Her ex husband met a sad fate, being inadvertently run over by a work colleague's tractor while he was taking an after lunch nap, unseen under a place of shade from the bright sunlight.

One day I had a phone call from my mother at work. She was in a very distraught state and asked me to go to my aunt's house because there was some terrible news. The son, Alexander, a young man of eighteen and a half, was dead. I received permission from my boss to go at once and when I got to the house I found the family understandably in a terrible state. Alexander was a lovely young man, tall and good looking, who reminded me of my father because of their visual likeness, When he was a young child he was very attached to my father and would go out of his way to do things to please him. One day when we were visiting, he went by tiptoe into my grandmother's room and produced a bottle of wine which he gave to my father! However, my grandmother had told me disturbing stories about him. He was in the habit of going into the woodshed, placing a bag over his heard and sniffing glue. This my grandmother had witnessed but his mother had done nothing to deal with this. At that time under the Soviet Union, all young men of 18 were called up to serve two years in the military and he was conscripted like the others. However, his drug addiction caused him to be kicked out of the army after a few months and he was sent home in disgrace. This was naturally a severe blow to his morale and he became withdrawn and depressed. That morning my grandmother had found him in the shed hanging from a rope with a bag over his head. A tragic waste of a young life which had so much promise, and that left behind a family wracked with grief.

The funeral was a big affair, he had lots of friends, one of whom was a young man named Vladimir who had been at school with him but was two years older. They had both come round to my flat one day to buy my vodka, which of course I let Alexander have for nothing. Marija hired a café for the day and paid for the refreshments for the large number that attended.

It took a long time to get over the shock of Alexander's death but after a few months I got the urge to have an evening out for a change. I have spoken about the large open air theatre that used to hold discos in the evening and it was the place to go to for a night out on warm summer evenings. A woman neighbour with whom I used to socialise now and again was also keen on the idea so we went along to see what was happening that night. Outside the ticket desk there were a number of food and drink stalls and we were looking around before deciding to go in when I heard a voice calling my name. It turned out to be Vladimir and we started talking. We were all agreed that the music did not seem up to much so we decided to go back to my flat and have some drinks instead. The children were fast asleep and we did not wake them up and settled down for some quiet food and drink. My neighbour did not stay long and we were left alone, sitting talking until about two or three o'clock. Vladimir was very respectful and did not make any advances to me, but his language was awful. Every other word was a swear word, and the Russian vocabulary is much richer in profanity than English, I can assure you. I asked him to tone down his language especially in front of the children and he did make an effort. Over the coming weeks, we met quite often, going for walks, to the local discos or just spending time in my flat. The children got on well with him. Vita in particular loved him and would sit on his knee, and at the age of around four and a half would tell him in all seriousness that when she was grown up she wanted to marry him. He always behaved impeccably with me and one night when we had had too much to drink we went to sleep together and woke up in the morning with our clothes on!

Eventually he said he wanted to marry me but I pointed out to him that I was nearly eleven years older than him, already had four children and did not want more. This was not enough to put him off as he told me that he would be happy to bring my children up as his own. He gradually wore down my resistance and I agreed to marry so we went to the register office to get the necessary paper work started. In those days you had to give notice and it was three months before you got the go ahead.

You were than given a card which entitled you to buy items required for the wedding like a ring and a wedding dress. Such things were in short supply in Latvia at the turn of the decade. I remember we went to Riga to buy the ring and made a lengthy and fruitless train journey to Minsk in Belarus to try to buy a wedding dress and I eventually had to settle for something that was not my first choice and we had to postpone the wedding for a month because of practical difficulties like this.

Before all this, it was also clear that Vladimir's family were very unhappy about is being together. His mother, aunt and grandmother in particular were dead set against it and confronted me about it. I was too old for him, had four children and would ruin his life were just some of the reasons. His family were I am sorry to say, like so many of the Latvian country people, uneducated peasants, brought up in ignorance and superstition and believing all kinds of medieval nonsense that the rest of civilised Europe had shaken off centuries ago. I only found our later, but apparently they had sought out the services of a woman in the nearby village of Dzelzava who had a reputation as a clairvoyant, sorceress or witch, whatever word you wish to use. They persuaded Vladimir's uncle, Nicolai, who was a policeman, to drive them to the village for a consultation with this woman. When they saw her, she was apparently slightly tipsy, and gave them each a spoonful of some noxious substance to drink, promising that she would cast a spell that would prevent our relationship from continuing. On the journey home they were all sick in the car. I found all this out later from Nicolai, who used to socialise with us occasionally and he insisted that he was only the driver, playing no part in this black magic conspiracy.

Coincidence or not, we started to have a run of bad luck. Vladimir had a job as a boiler attendant at the municipal heating works, which supplied hot water and central heating of a sort to many of the town's population. One morning, he opened the boiler front door as normal to stoke it but was badly singed by a sudden burst of hot air and steam. He lost his eyebrows, some hair and his face was badly scalded but fortunately the ambulance crew arrived very quickly and treated his injuries promptly so no lasting damage was done, although it was obviously a very painful experience. A short time later, Vita was bitten by a dog in the street and had to be treated in hospital.

Hearing of these events, a friend of mine put me in touch with someone who was reputed to be a white witch, a gipsy woman from Variklani who would counteract the malign spells of the other woman so we went to see her and had separate audiences with her. The upshot was that she promised us that only death would separate us.

His family continued to try to separate us. I found out from a friend who worked in the register office that his aunt had tried to find out in a phone call about our wedding date but had been given short shrift as she was not entitled to know about private information. On the wedding day we had many of my work colleagues and other friends and relatives as guests but no one from his family of course. The adults were in one room and the children in another which was where the phone was. When it rang Olga answered it and it was Vladimir's mother. She asked to speak to her son and Olga told her it was not possible. She asked why and Olga told her because we were having a wedding feast. His mother exploded at this news and Olga burst into the room crying to tell us what had happened. Valdimir went to the phone and a heated exchange of words took place ending with her saying she cursed him and Vladimir telling her he was no longer her son. Everyone was very upset, the children were crying and it was a sad end to what was up, until her intervention, a happy occasion.

From then on he had no contact with his family but shortly before his birthday the following year, he had a phone call from his mother, lamenting the fact that she was missing him and asking if they could pay us a visit for his birthday. I was of course very much against this as I knew it would spell trouble but on the other hand it was his family and perhaps things would be different this time as we had been married for a few months and time might have softened their opposition to me. So, on 29

March they duly arrived and what a thoroughly miserable occasion it turned out to be. Ten of them came. Their eyes were everywhere, looking into every little detail of our life together. Little, or no conversation with the women while his father, an alcoholic, got steadily the worse for wear and finally capped a horrible day when he staggered to his feet and announced "You have stolen my son. You must have a golden pussy". I use a politer version of the language he used. Enough to say that he was a very good teacher as far as his son was concerned in his use of the most obscene words in the Russian language.

After this very unpleasant occasion things settled down on a day to day basis. I still had my job at the sanitation office, still had my private customers for the rat poison and the vodka, although the latter was slowing down somewhat. I continued to make the regular trips to Poland to bring in extra income. Our social life did not amount to much, we had a few regular visitors including Nicolai, Vladimir's uncle, who, as I have said, was a policeman but also well known as an inveterate womaniser. He seemed to be always around our flat and whenever he had the chance, used to try to corner me on my own and tell me how I was far too good for his nephew, that Vladimir was an idiot, far too young for me and that he wanted to marry me. He was prepared to leave his wife if I would go away with him etc etc.   I tried to brush this off   but he persisted in phoning me.   Finally, I told Vladimir about his unwanted attention but he just laughed it off, refusing to believe it.

Vladimir's mother's parents had a house in the depths of the country where they had lots of land. April was the time of year for planting potatoes, grown principally for feeding themselves, and more importantly the pigs they kept, who had an enormous appetite. Her parents were quite old and needed some help so one day we all set off to their place on foot, which was several kilometres, to get the job done.   They had previously had the ground semi prepared by having a tractor plough up the field but this was still a major operation.   It was a vast field and had to be ploughed into furrows and it fell to me to drag the hand plough behind me up and down supported by the men, who included Nicolai and Vladimir's father.   The women followed on, planting the potatoes and then of course we had to repeat the exercise by filling in the soil along the rows we had ploughed.   It was an exhausting day's work.   At least I received some praise from Vladimir's father, who was quite scathing about the lack of effort on the part of his womenfolk compared to my efforts, and from then on, things were a little better between us.   There were a few rows left over and I was allowed to plant some beetroot and cucumber seeds for our own use as a reward for my labours, but later I never had so much as one cucumber as the grandparents made use of them.

CHAPTER 10

During the autumn of 1993 I discovered I was pregnant. We had not intended to have any children as I have said, four being quite enough, but after a lot of soul searching and discussion, we decided to go ahead. I recall that during this pregnancy I had many a strange fancy. I craved for cream cakes and sweets, was thrilled by the smell of diesel fumes from passing buses and although I had never smoked, loved the smell of tobacco so much that I used to stick one of Vladimir's cigarettes behind my ear so that its fragrance stayed with me all day. I also loved beer, but limited myself to keeping one bottle in the fridge from which I would have very small amounts of about 50 ml at a time. The old women used to say I was sure to have a girl.

I was able to leave my job on maternity leave two months before the birth and even in my condition Nicolai continued to pester me as before which by now was becoming a real bore, but I was able to brush him off easily as there was never the remotest chance of him succeeding. I gave birth to a son on 12th May 1994, with the usual problems with the placenta but apart from that, all was straightforward. One day at the hospital I had a visit from Vladimir and his mother, who complimented me on how quickly I had regained my figure. They wanted to call our son Vitaly, which was not a name I would have chosen, but I gave in to their appeals for the sake of peace and quiet and the hope that it might make relations between us a bit better. At least his family had stopped trying to break us up but unfortunately our own relationship was starting to hit the rocks.

He had recently changed jobs and was now working in forestry, an occupation that was and still is, the mainstay of the local economy. Chopping down trees and then processing them in to logs was an arduous but well paid job. The hours were long and he left home at 6am and returned twelve hours later. Some nights he stayed with work mates at their houses in the forest. One Friday he came home early saying that he was going to go out drinking with his friends. I was standing near a wall with Vitaly, who was only a few weeks old, in my arms and told him that it was no good him doing this as I had to go out and get some shopping for food and could not leave Vitaly alone or take him with me. Vladimir would have to look after him. He became very aggressive and in the course of the argument, pushed me with both hands as hard as he could against the wall. My back hit hard against the wall, and I slowly slid down onto the bench which was against it, somehow holding on to Vitaly. This was very fortunate and I do not like to think what might have happened if I had let him fall on to the hard concrete floor. Vladimir stormed out of the house, only returning on Sunday. When he did, we of course had a big row, but he told me how sorry he was and that it would not happen again etc. but this had set a pattern for what was to follow.

We had not got a car at this stage and with five young children it was becoming a necessity for getting about so we bought an old Moskvich which soon broke down and proved to be beyond repair. My boss at work sold us a newer version which was fine. Vladimir had learned to drive while doing his army service but I was not a driver at this stage. We were able to go out to the beautiful lakes and forests that surround Madona and our lives were opened up to wider possibilities than being cooped up in a flat all day.

This was at weekends of course because Vladimir was working long hours as I have said. During the week I would see occasional visitors including a woman who lived in the block and worked for the local authority in a big white office building in the centre of Madona. This woman had a drinking habit which caused her to go missing from her work from time to time but she used to call on me for a chat and a drink now and again. One day when I was alone in my flat, her boss knocked on my door, enquiring if the lady in question was with me. I was not at all happy at her manner or presumption in knocking on my door, and the following day was even less impressed when she turned up again, this time flanked by three policemen to make the same enquiry, especially as her quarry was actually in my flat at the time! The woman attempted to step inside but I thrust out my arm to prevent her and asked her by what authority she presumed to enter my flat. Was she in possession of a warrant? Behind her, I could see the policemen quietly smiling to themselves. Eventually they departed empty handed and we had a good laugh about it. When she went back to work the next day her boss mentioned my part in protecting her and henceforth I was given the nickname 'The Advocate' by which name I was known in the future in that department.

Although we were renting our flat from the local authority rather than being property owners, there existed in Latvia, and no doubt still does, an unofficial market, to put it diplomatically, whereby money would change hands. If for example, you wanted to downsize from a three bed flat to a one bed apartment you could find someone willing to swap and that person would pay you money in exchange. We had found a bungalow for sale with a large garden which was ideal for our purposes and the owner was a woman who I discovered was someone I used to go to school with. This was fortunate as she was very cooperative in the period leading up to the completion. In order to raise the necessary money to buy the property we had to go through the following process:

Find someone interested in taking on our 3 bed flat who had a 1 bed flat and was willing to exchange.

Agree a price (unofficially of course as far as the local authority was concerned). Move into the one bed flat for a month while finding someone who wanted to take this over from us.

Once that was achieved, take the money from our first flat, the money from the second one, add some of my clothes business funds and pay for the bungalow.

So it happened that we moved into the bungalow where we had much more room and enough land to become largely self sufficient, growing vegetables and keeping two pigs and our lives should have been stable and happy. When sober, Vladimir was hard working in the garden and in improving the bungalow. It was on the underside of a hill and he constructed a ditch which took away the rainwater which otherwise would have caused us problems and built a little bridge over it to get to the front door. He also built an underground smokehouse from which we enjoyed delicious chicken dinners and other tasty delights.

Unfortunately he fell into bad company working in the forests. The loggers were nearly all heavy drinkers with rough and ready ways and lived a tough life, working in temperatures often 35 degrees below in the winter. They had big open fires to keep warm, sitting around and drinking home brewed vodka made from the forest berries, but they were all very experienced in this way of life and knew how far to go. Vladimir was by comparison an innocent in this environment, apt to sit too near the fire and not realise he was almost burning because he was so cold and trying to get warm. On another occasion he was cutting into a tree at the wrong angle with his chainsaw as a result of which the tree fell towards him rather than away, and he was lucky it was only the outer branches that grazed him rather than the main trunk falling on him.

Many times he brought home vodka when he was already drunk and I used to tip it down the sink. One day he came home when the snow was very deep outside and I became suspicious that it took him so long to get to the front door and come in. When he eventually did, he was dead drunk and went straight to bed. I went outside and had a look round and saw a dark colour amid the whiteness of the snow. It was the top of a vodka bottle which he had hidden away from me! I telephoned my friend Anna, and she came round to share it with me. In the morning he did not even remember what he had done with the missing vodka, searching for it high and low, but when he discovered the empty bottle he understood.

To mark Women's Day, March 8, the loggers were given a bounty so that they could buy gifts for their womenfolk but they had to be transported in a lorry to the depot to receive this money in cash. The driver was in his cab and the men were accommodated in the back of the covered in lorry where there were two rows of seats separated by a central aisle. There were windows to look out of but it was a long journey of a couple of hours during which the vodka was flowing, of course. Having collected the money the lorry driver then stopped to enable the men to buy their presents to take home. Vladimir bought some perfume and creams in a box which he placed in his rucksack, unfortunately not closing the zip. During the journey home, the lorry had to stop for the calls of nature to be answered after a serious bout of drinking, so the company stepped out into the deep snow by the forest road. One of the men noticed that Vladimir's rucksack was open and told him, and to his horror he realised the box containing his present to me was lost. He eventually found it under the snow and obviously it was very wet, and got in a worse condition as the journey wore on.

When he did not arrive home at the expected time I began to worry and after a while I telephoned one of the men I knew was on the same lorry and he told me they had been home for a while. The driver had been driving round the town trying to find where to drop Vladimir off and I went out in the road to flag him down. It was bitterly cold and the snow was deep. The driver opened the back of the lorry, and there was my husband, flat out on his back between the aisles of seats. I tried to revive him and his first words were 'What are you doing in the forest?' I helped him to his feet and tried to hold him up but there were several steps down from the back of the lorry to the road and oblivious to this he stepped out into the blackness and fell onto the snow below. Expecting the worst, I was surprised when he stood up almost immediately, obviously so drunk with his body so completely relaxed that he suffered no injury from the fall. He proudly gave me my present, in a dripping wet, soggy cardboard box but at least the contents were not damaged.

One day in the market in the town we came across an alcoholic with a mongrel puppy dog on a string that was all skin and bone. The dog was in a bad way and we discovered that in order to combat worms, the owner had fed him vodka with some peppers which had made him sick. We bought the dog for 1 rouble and took him home, where he very soon recovered with a good diet and soon became a very welcome addition to the household who we called Dika. Vladimir made him a kennel but in the very cold weather he slept in the wood store. Like most of the dogs in Madona he was kept mainly as a guard dog and it was customary for such dogs to be kept on a chain for most of the time which is quite different of course from the way British people keep their pets.

As I have said, we kept a couple of pigs and with a glut of apples one year I fed them to the pigs. The next day there were a lot of pink objects on the ground in their area and on inspection, these proved to be worms. Until then, we had no idea how effective apples were in getting rid of worms. Vladimir's father had all the equipment necessary to slaughter and butcher pigs so every year we used to replace the two adults with two piglets.

I had stopped producing vodka and also no longer went to Poland but an acquaintance put me in touch with a wholesaler in Riga who could supply me with a wide range of clothes to set up my stock as I had a lengthy list of customers from my previous efforts. In the meantime, Vladimir had plans to build an extension to the bungalow that would provide another room and most importantly, an indoor toilet. After enduring trips to an outside toilet in the depths of a Latvian winter for so long, this was a luxury to look forward to.

CHAPTER 11

My mother, as I have written, was a woman who was self contained and not given to showing her feelings. Her mother was the same and unlike my father's family, they did not express their views vociferously. I suppose it shows up the differences between stereotypical national characteristics – Russians passionately declaiming their views and beliefs for all to hear, Latvians quiet and undemonstrative and giving nothing away. She had met her new man friend Peter when I was still a teenager about nine months or so after my father died. I was going to a disco at the usual open air venue with my friend Natalya and persuaded my mother to come out for the evening as it would do her good. We arrived at the venue and took seats as we waited for the music to start. When it did, this man came up to my mother and asked her to dance. They hit it off and began to start meeting occasionally until one day when I went to see her he had moved in. This did not go down well with my father's relatives who resented that it was less than a year since my father had died and was against their Russian customs, which stipulated that it had to be at least a year before a widow or widower could take on a new relationship and things were never quite the same between them after this.
He had a sizeable farm in the village of Murmanstiene which was some distance away,

where he kept bees for honey which he sold together with pigs, cows, sheep, poultry and many vegetables so the majority of his time was spent there. What I discovered later was that he was already married and had left his wife, who was a bus conductress, when he discovered that she was having an affair with the bus driver behind his back, something which was common knowledge around the town, rendering him a laughing stock.

When I came back to Madona she had been in a relationship with this man for the intervening years. Moving into her small flat with my children was a very uncomfortable experience for all of us but as I have explained it was for about a month while the problem with the tenants in my flat was being resolved. I must say how helpful she was to me at this time as I had returned to Madona with virtually nothing and somehow she managed to provide me with all sorts of basic household things ranging from cutlery to dishes to clothes for the children, as did my grandmothers as well. However, she told me she had been diagnosed as diabetic but I could never establish just what medication she was on or whether she was taking it as instructed as she was very secretive about the details. I was also shocked one day to discover a box of about thirty bottles of cologne and when I asked her what this was all about she told me to mind my own business. I have already mentioned her drink problem and although I never knew for certain, I believe she used to drink this cologne, which contained alcohol. I knew that in Madona, a number of homeless people used to drink this as a cheap substitute for vodka as one day in the town I was accosted by a beggar who asked me to buy him some.

My mother left her job when she reached the age of 55, receiving a pension. She began to spend time at Peter's farm and one Friday, she took the bus to the village, laden down with a couple of heavy bags of shopping. The bus dropped her off at the nearest point and she now had to walk a distance to the farm, a journey down an uncomfortable, dusty gravel track. Her boots were only thin and unfortunately, a stone pierced though the sole and then dug into her heel. This was obviously very dangerous for a diabetic, and an infection started which became serious and she had to go into hospital. Gangrene set in and her left leg had to be amputated just below the knee. She was fitted with a prosthetic lower leg and given a wheel chair.

By now, we were living in our bungalow and I used to cook for her and send the children with food deliveries to her flat. Doctors had told her to stop drinking and to improve her diet. Sadly, she loved fat meat, salted preferably in common with many of my compatriots who were brought up on such food and it was hard for her to change her habits. It was becoming very difficult to see she was properly cared for. Peter was only occasionally with her now when he was in Madona and it was known that he was seeing his wife as well, although she did not know this. I decided that the best thing was for her to come and live with us so that I could look after her properly, although we hardly had the room. She rarely went out and on one occasion when she did, she fell over on the pavement on the way back from a nearby shop and had to be helped up by some neighbours. She had gone out to buy a bottle. Eventually she agreed to come and stay with us but despite my good intentions it proved to be a disaster. The cramped conditions, the children playing music at times and needing their quiet times for homework etc all led to tensions and she was not taking her tablets regularly, just sleeping and sleeping and crying that she had nothing to live for. Peter had made her a commode and she was always in need of it and I used to have to get the children to help me lift her on and off as Vladimir worked such long hours in the forest and was seldom on hand when needed.

Eventually it was decided that Peter would take her to the farm and I used to visit her every week. Each time I saw her, she was worse. She was becoming bloated – swollen legs, arms body, face and sleeping most of the time and it was decided we needed to take her to the hospital. While waiting for a doctor, she was asleep at first but then woke up and asked where she was. On being told I will never forget her words 'I shall never leave here'. She was put in the intensive care unit and for the next few days was very drowsy and slow to speak. She lapsed into a coma and the next time I saw her she was unrecognisable as my mother. She was grotesquely swollen and cold to the touch and it was obvious her time was short. Driving home, I had to stop the car several times as my eyes were filled with tears at what had become of my mother. The next morning, a neighbour, who worked at the hospital, called round to break the news to me that my mother had died. She was just 60 years of age.

Looking back, I wish I could change things. If only I had been more pressing about her diagnosis, about her medication, about how to manage her condition and all the other things I could have done to prevent her dying so young.

CHAPTER 12

Our bungalow was work in progress during these years. It was on a large site with ample land for what we wanted, and as I have said Vladimir was very hard working on improvements around the place. The woman we had bought it from had lived there with her parents before she married and moved away. They were old people and alcoholics who ended up in either a nursing home or hospital where they died, so the bungalow had been empty for two years. It was in a terrible state with thin walls, a roof that would not survive many more hard Latvian winters and the garden such as it was, was strewn with all kinds of rubbish, broken tools, bits of machinery and fragments of glass and was a dangerous place for children. The *piece de resistance* however was the outside toilet. Obviously it was not connected to the main sewage system but at least we expected it to have a septic tank of some sort which would be emptied by the local authority on a regular basis. No, on investigation, nothing, just a hole in the ground. Vladimir dug a trench and cleaned things up as best he could, but apart from the unpleasant nature of the job, he also found numerous skulls of dogs, hedgehogs and other animals among the rubbish.

With the help of a man who he worked with in the forest and who was a good builder, at weekends Vladimir began work on extending the bungalow with an inside toilet and additional room, amounting to about fifty square metres and in addition, an extra layer of good quality bricks and a new roof for good measure. This was a job that took all summer. As well as this, they also levelled the ground at the front in preparation for a garage.

The bungalow seemed to have an identity of its own. Often I would lie awake at night and hear all sorts of strange sounds, rustling, tapping, scratching, probably birds or mice, but I did begin to wonder if it was haunted by some restless spirit. Nevertheless, we were beginning to make it more like we wanted it as the years went by. Round about the time Vitaly was four years old, my kitchen stove needed replacement and we were put in touch with a man who was allegedly an expert in these matters. He built us a wood burner with a top for cooking and when he finished the job, I paid him his money and was looking forward to the next day when I had planned to do a lot of washing. Vladimir went outside to get buckets of water in preparation to fill our pans and bathtubs etc and when he came in, mentioned that he could smell something burning. The wall behind the new stove was red hot and something was clearly wrong. Vladimir rushed outside, grabbed a ladder and climbed up on to the roof where there was access to the loft though a trap door, a common feature of Latvian roofs. On climbing in, he discovered the loft was full of smoke. We hurriedly vacated the bungalow, grabbing some possessions as best we could and called the fire brigade. While we were waiting I suddenly realised that although the two girls were with us, there was no Vitaly. I rushed back inside and there he was, sitting in front of the television screen with his headphones on, watching a video and entirely oblivious to what was going on around him. The fire crew arrived in a very short time and put out the fire promptly without too much damage, apart from some water which came though the ceiling and was an inevitable consequence. We were very grateful to the fire fighters and gave them some bottles and sweets for their efforts.

A neighbour offered to look after Vitaly for the night, friends who had acted as witnesses at our wedding put up Vladimir and Olga but I elected to stay in the bungalow with Vita, not wishing to leave it. I barely slept that night, hearing lots of strange noises, probably on reflection the sound of water still trickling down the walls, but I cannot forget what I saw that night – a shadowy figure who appeared in the open door – a sight that made my hairs stand on end but which left me too paralysed with fright to get up and investigate.

In the morning the police called and we gave them the full information about the man who had fitted my new stove. We learned later that he was arrested and appeared in court charged with negligence for failing to properly insulate the stove with asbestos and causing the fire which resulted and he was made to pay for the cost of the fire brigade attending the fire, and fined a penalty as well but I never received any compensation for the trouble he had caused us. He was also prohibited from undertaking any such work in future but I suspect he did not adhere to this court order after a suitable time had elapsed. In the meantime, we only had a fire in the other living room and until we had a replacement stove life was uncomfortable.

As a postscript, our dog Dika soon had a companion. A woman who worked at the police station contacted me to say that one of their police dogs had recently had a litter of puppies and they were looking for homes for them and was I interested? Of course I was, having always liked German Shepherd dogs, so we acquired a month old puppy who soon grew into a large animal who gave us a lot of pleasure. We named him Tom. On the night before the fire, a neighbour called me to say that both our dogs, who were in the garden, were howling and that this foretold a death. The same night, I had a dream that our woodshed was on fire and I was rushing to put out the fire with bucket load after bucket load of water and there was smoke billowing everywhere. Coincidence or prophesy, who knows, but all these years later, such things still go through my mind.

CHAPTER 13

I need to backtrack a bit now to bring my daughter Liana's story up to date. As the oldest of my children she was a very capable and efficient surrogate mother as she became older. She was a good cook, kept the house clean and tidy and looked after the children well and when I made my monthly trips to Poland I knew that at fourteen years of age I could rely on her. There were never any adverse comments from my neighbours about her when I came back and I was really proud of her. One day on my return from Poland she had prepared chicken soup for me, knowing that I had not had a hot meal all week. I tucked into this and it was delicious but I was disconcerted to find a small scrap of paper in the middle. Normally I am very fastidious about finding foreign bodies in my food, even a small hair would put me off finishing the meal, but knowing the trouble she had gone to I carried on eating, not wishing to disappoint or upset her. However, she noticed that I had found this piece of paper and asked if everything was ok. It turned out that she had taken the chicken out of the freezer the previous night but had not washed it, not realising that that was required. There were no after effects despite this and everyone was happy.
She was very mature for her age in many ways and began to get restless at school. She also started going to discos and meeting boys and this was

putting a strain on life at home. When she was fifteen or so she wanted to leave her school and enrol at a cookery college. She also decided she wanted to live with her father in his flat as he had a spare bedroom and I guess she thought that she would have more independence that way. When she moved into his flat he had other ideas and forced her back to school for a further term and she was worse off, because he gave her nothing in the way of money to spend on herself that young girls of that age need.

An event occurred next which underlined how malicious my first husband Vladimir's mother had become. As if my current mother in law was not causing enough problems, this woman was still angling to get her son back with me and invented a complete fabrication designed to split up me and Vladimir 2, as I shall refer to him in this chapter. She persuaded Liana to go with her to the police station and report that Vladimir 2 had tried to molest her, and statements were taken. The next day Vladimir 2 and I were summoned to the police station to hear the charges against him and we in turn made statements denying anything of the kind had ever happened. Perhaps it was fortunate that we were both well known to several of the officers in the station as they were customers of my clothing business and were regular visitors to our house. The result was that no charges were made and nothing further came of it but the scars took a long time to heal, especially my daughter's part in this fantasy. Vladimir 2 was a decent, straightforward, hard working man whose downfall was to be his alcoholism but I would never accuse him, or believe him to be guilty of anything like this. When we were done at the police office we went to her father's flat and called out these false accusers so that their neighbours knew all about it.

After a short time, this same grandmother arranged Liana to join a college near Riga where she could study cookery and board there during the week, coming home at weekends. This worked out fine for a couple of years or so and when her course was finished she was all set to start work.

In the meantime she had begun a relationship with a young man and now had become pregnant. We discussed the options and I stressed that it was up to her but pointed out that she had her life in front of her and it seemed like history was repeating itself with regard to my early life and my mother's. Her decision after much thought and discussion with the doctor was to have an abortion. Sadly, the result of this was that she was subsequently unable to have children and it was a decision that still comes back to haunt her and myself as well, although in the end it was up to her.

She got a job in the canteen of the local authority building providing food and drink for the workers there and she started living with her boyfriend. It turned out to be an abusive relationship as he frequently beat her and left her badly bruised. She left him after less than a year and we put her up in the bungalow for a while but this was not working out. She had a friend in Germany who invited her to go there to live and work and this she decided to do.

She soon settled there, in Dusseldorf, and one day I received a letter telling me she was going to get married and asking me to come as she wanted some of her family there as her husband had a large family and she did not want to be completely outnumbered. Vitaly was now about two years old so Olga stayed behind with Vladimir to look after him while I went with Vita, a trip that would last only a few days. Liana made a lovely bride and we had a nice time. Her husband was a Turk, and at the reception there was no alcohol, which made a nice change. His family were very friendly and pleasant to us and the next day we met again at their place for lunch and enjoyed it.

One of the things I remember most about this trip was that the newly weds had a beautiful Rottweiler dog. One morning we were sleeping when I became aware of hot breath and a large face in front of me trying to wake me up. Liana could not be roused and the poor dog was desperate for a walk to go to the toilet, running up and down the flat in an increasingly anxious state. He went so far as to bring me his collar and lead! I hurriedly dressed and took him out, together with Vita, and we had a great time. The next day we took the bus home, a long journey that took many hours as we left Germany, travelling through Poland and eventually back home to Madona.

Certain distressing events back home, which I will recount later, had somewhat clouded the happy events of our trip but that is for another day. Suffice to say that I was happy for my eldest daughter that she had found happiness.

CHAPTER 14

I now need to spend some time writing a bit about Sergei, my eldest son, who was born in 1979. When I went back to work after maternity leave, this was at the electrical manufacturers in Madona where my start time was 6am. While Liana was looked after by my husband's mother during the week, including staying there at night, my maternal grandfather used to come to our flat and look after Sergei, arriving at 5.30 in the morning so that I had time to get to work.

Sergei was very late learning to talk and in fact did not utter a word in his first few years. We spoke Russian at home but his grandfather, as I have explained before, spoke only Latvian, so communication was difficult between them.   I eventually consulted the doctor about him and it was established that he could understand everything that was said to him in both Russian and Latvian but was either unable or unwilling to speak. One day, when he was about three, much to our surprise he began to speak and it was impossible after that to get him to stop as he suddenly discovered the power of speech. He was a good little boy on the whole but he often clashed with Liana when they were playing with their toys. One day I was working in the kitchen when I heard a loud cry from the next room and rushed in to find Liana standing their with blood streaming down her face from a cut on her forehead and Sergei standing with a plastic bucket in his hand which he had hit her with in an argument over a particular toy. I was so cross I snatched the bucket from him and whacked him around the head with it, causing him to have an identical cut on his forehead to the one he had inflicted on his sister. I could make the excuse of an inexperienced young mother under pressure but regretted this immediately and was very upset.

Another thing I remember from those early days was a lovely suit of clothes I bought Sergei, mustard coloured velvet jacket and trousers with a matching gilet. The first day he wore it we went shopping together and we were a long time out of doors. Walking home with the bags of shopping we were about to pass a large puddle on the pavement when Sergei suddenly started to cry, got down on his knees in the puddle and needing to go to the toilet, wet himself inside and out, as well as ruining the lovely new clothes. Needless to say, he received a good telling off, but I should perhaps have anticipated that being out a long time, he might have needed the toilet. Inexperience again on my part.

One day when they were both very young I sent Liana and Sergei to a shop very near to the flat with a list of things to get. She was going to pick up the items from the shelf and he was following behind her. Liana paid for the shopping but as they were about to leave the store a security guard intercepted them and took them to a small room where they were quizzed about shoplifting. She knew nothing about it and produced the receipt for them to check the goods, but unbeknown to her, Sergei had been picking up sweets and putting them in the hood of her coat, which was hanging behind her. She had felt him tugging at her back, but thought he was just messing about! The store manager recognised the children and promptly telephoned Vladimir, who was at the shop in five minutes and promptly frogmarched the children back to my flat where he gave Sergei a good belting and promised Liana that his mother would have a few words with her when she got home.

I managed to get both Liana and Sergei into kindergarten before too long and by now I was divorced from Vladimir and had started my relationship with Pavel. We were shortly to depart for Siberia and there is little to tell about those years from the childrens' point of view so I will now move forward to our return to Madona.

When they started school there they both proved good scholars, quick to learn and diligent enough with their studies. There always used to be arguments between them when they started on their homework and I used to supervise this in a strict manner. So strict in fact that Sergei once said I would have made a good Gestapo officer during the war!

He was often in trouble at school. One such incident has stayed with me because of its sheer absurdity. In the school there was a room leading off a corridor where there was a music centre for playing records at times during the day, which would be transmitted though loudspeakers in the corridors. The door to this room was always open and one day in break time Sergei went into the room and grabbed about thirty single discs, stuffing them in his school bag, down his shirt front and anywhere else he could hide them. Going back into the class room he distributed them to his classmates. The head teacher became aware of the missing records and went from class to class to investigate. On entering Sergei's classroom and making his inquiries he was no doubt astonished at the response from most of the pupils flourishing their records which my son had kindly dished out to all and sundry. I was contacted by the school about the matter but my answer was it had happened under their jurisdiction and had been resolved so what did they expect or want me to do about it? Obviously I questioned Sergei but he never gave me an explanation, his bottom lip firmly jutting out in defiance.

Unfortunately, these minor misdemeanours at school started to escalate into more serious matters and his teenage years were a recurring story of anti social behaviour, hooliganism of various kinds from breaking windows to hanging about in gangs and being a nuisance to the public. He seemed unable to keep out of trouble and his activities brought him to the notice of the childrens' unit of the local police, where Vladimir 2's aunt, Irena, worked. Part of her duties involved visiting the homes of these problematic children to assess the conditions they were living in and she duly made arrangements to inspect us. I was gratified that we passed the test with flying colours in all respects – cleanliness, facilities, accommodation etc and she told me that our home was in marked contrast to some of the homes she had to visit. This made it all the more difficult to explain Sergei's wayward behaviour as he wanted for nothing. Perhaps it was simply heredity. His father was a shiftless, hopeless alcoholic like his father before him. He was a personable young man, intelligent enough and instantly likeable but he could not be helped.

Womens' Day is a big occasion in Latvia and I have already mentioned the ill fated attempt by Vladimir one year to buy me some perfume, but he always tried to put money aside in the early months of the year to buy me a nice present as well as the obligatory flowers. Sergei started to go missing sometimes and on one occasion when he had been gone three days, Vladimir realised that his savings money had disappeared. Shortly after, Irena had been tipped off about a major discovery. Deep in the bowels of a certain block of flats, there was a boiler room that apparently the gang of lads of which Sergei was a member had appropriated for their use as a den for gambling, drinking and whatever else. They would sleep there as they chose, which explained Sergei's frequent disappearances. They were caught red handed and there was a lot of drink there, many unopened bottles and cans.

Things went from bad to worse. One day he brought home about fifteen bottles of liqueurs, wines and spirits and had no explanation where he got them from. I kept them together intact in a separate place in case there should be an enquiry about them. On leaving school, he started work on and off in the forest. One day, on leaving work he broke into a nearby house on the off chance and stole a computer on the hope of selling it. He was traced by the police and received a two year prison sentence. This pattern was to repeat itself over the next few years with two more convictions for petty theft. Worse was to come when an abortive robbery at a grocery store went wrong. Among the items stolen were some sachets of mayonnaise, which during the getaway started to ooze out on the ground and on to the clothes of the thieves, leading the police to pick up the trail quite easily. They caught one of the gang, who to improve his chances of leniency, shopped the rest of them, including Sergei. Before he could be arrested,

Sergei found out what had happened, confronted his betrayer with a knife, slashing him several times in the back. He had graduated from pranks at school to hooliganism and petty theft to violence and for this he went down for four and a half years.

CHAPTER 15

When I came to write this book I imaged a straightforward chronicle, moving forward, year by year in a smooth unbroken flow. I soon realised that as in life, progress is not always linear and that sometimes the past has to be revisited from different angles and perspectives in order to make sense of it all. A writer of fiction is able to order events of his or her own choosing, an autobiography is much more complex to organise and sometimes one has to go back and approach subjects from a different view point to previous references.

Thus I now return to the narrative which was interrupted by my reflections on the early years of my two oldest children, Liana and Sergei. My business activities were going well, selling clothes and other items to my increasing number of contacts both in Madona and in the surrounding villages but I was hampered by two main problems. Firstly, I did not drive and relied upon an old school friend, Oleg, to drive me to Riga to pick up my supplies from the wholesaler. He was always as helpful as he could be, but sometimes it was not convenient for him. Secondly, we had a car at home which Vladimir did not use for work as he was taken there by bus. During the summer, because of the unpleasantly hot conditions in the forest plus insects being a nuisance, he would start work at perhaps four o'clock in the morning and be home at two. This in theory would enable him to drive me round the numerous villages where I had customers, who I would have previously advised of the dates I would be calling. Unfortunately, he was not a reliable chauffeur, often too drunk to drive. I made up my mind that it was about time I learnt to drive so I duly enrolled for lessons. In Latvia, this was a fairly intensive three month schedule of practical lessons and classroom lectures. I often went to bed with a copy of the prescribed textbook in my hand and did my best to memorise as much as I could. The big day arrived for my test, along with all the other members of my class and it involved both a practical and a written test. I passed with a 100% mark and as one of the oldest in the class, this was particularly pleasing. Unlike in England, where you are just told if you have passed or not, the results were made public before my fellow learners, and I left the centre feeling very pleased with myself. I rang Vladimir to tell him my good news and was looking forward to getting home and having a nice evening to celebrate my success with a couple of drinks and hopefully a bunch of flowers. I arrived home to an empty house and my mood of euphoria, not for the first or indeed the last time was abruptly punctured. Needless to say, he had been out drinking and was very sorry the next day etc.

My driving licence came through in March 2000. Our old Moskvitch was now unreliable and having sold it we had to find a car. One of Vladimir's friends who had been a witness at our wedding accompanied us to Riga in his car to help us choose a suitable vehicle and we finally settled on an Audi 80 costing about £3000 in today's money. His friend was something of a car expert and ran the rule over it for us. Despite that, it proved to be a bit of a money trap in the future as every month we were spending money on repairs so I suppose the moral of the story is never trust an expert! At the time though, we were very pleased with it. Having completed the deal I then realised that I would have to drive it home and we were on the far side of Riga, meaning I would have my first solo outing at the wheel negotiating the country's capital city's streets followed by a three hour drive to get home. Vladimir's friend was asked to drive slowly in front of us in case I had any problems. Vladimir himself was a nervous passenger but it was my car and I had to do it, despite the intimidating nature of the journey. Happily we arrived back in Madona without any incident, until we reached our road only to find there was a 'no entry' sign in the middle of the road. Puzzled by this, I drove round the block to approach our bungalow from a different direction only to find that there was another 'no entry' sign that side as well. We got out of the car to investigate what this was all about when our five immediate neighbours and their families came out of their houses, cheering and clapping us and presenting me with flowers. This was a lovely and heart warming gesture and they were all invited in for an evening of eating, drinking and celebrating. I found out about the road signs: one of our neighbours had kept them in his greenhouse for years.

We were very fortunate with our neighbours, all nice people who were friendly and helpful towards each other. We were always exchanging produce from our gardens and in and out of each others houses for various celebrations. I mentioned before that our garden was a disgrace when we first moved in but Vladimir had worked hard to transform it. The soil was heavy clay, but we got in several car loads of good quality soil and mixed it in and then after planting obtained a large barrel of poultry droppings from the nearby chicken farm. One of the things we grew attracted great interest from our neighbours. Our courgettes were something to behold, growing into huge leafy plants with a yield that caused one neighbour to say that she had never seen anything like it in all her years.

Back to my new car, this enabled me to have freedom and independence so that my clothes business developed quite rapidly. Every Friday I would have new stock from Riga, a journey I was now quite happy to make, and when I got back there were often customers at my door waiting for my return. However, just as everything was going so well, a small disaster struck. I wrote previously about my trip to Germany for Liana's wedding, accompanied by Vita, leaving Olga and Vitaly in the charge of my husband. As my previous reference was all about my daughter Liana, I chose not to mention the next events in order to keep the focus on her, but what happened was as follows.

Olga rang me from home the day after the wedding to say that Vladimir had come home the night before, stripped the fridge of all the food despite her protestations and driven off in the car. She was able to borrow some money from a friend to buy food for herself and Vitaly but Vladimir had not returned that night.

Later, I discovered what had happened. Already the worse for drink, he had taken two of his workmates to a remote village where they, along with more than ten others, were going to stay at a woman's house, drink and have sex with her, one after the other. Near their destination, on a gravel track, because he was driving so recklessly under the influence, he rolled the car, it turned over several times, his two passengers were hurled through the windscreen but he only suffered minor cuts and bruises. One of the men lived quite nearby and later was able to get an ambulance to take him to hospital, claiming he had fallen off a roof! The car was towed away by a friend of

Vladimir and taken to their garden and hidden away. It was obviously going to be out of action for some time to come.

While still in Germany, I was able to get help from Liana's husband. He arranged for me to buy a VW Passat for delivery back home in a couple of weeks.

When I got back home Vladimir was not there so I got Oleg to drive me to where he was working and he was not there either, a colleague telling me that he had left for home a while before. . By now I was getting near boiling point and as we were quite near where this woman lived I asked for directions and we arrived there shortly. I did not wait to knock on the door but went straight in where she standing in front of a table with glass jars on it where she was preparing some preserves. Without standing on ceremony, I punched her right between the eyes as hard as I could and then swept all the glass jars off the table. When I got back to the car, I was shaking like a leaf and blood spattered. Oleg could see I was upset and said not a word as we drove home while I gradually regained my composure. When we got home Vladimir was there and I told him to pack his bags and go to this woman. It was the usual story – he was drunk and didn't mean it to happen to which I answered he was not drunk when he took the food from the fridge and upset the children, and that it had all been planned.

The next day he went back to work and a colleague later told me what happened on the bus. The woman was also on the bus, sporting two black eyes and with numerous cuts on her face. When she saw him she uttered a few choice words, adding that had she known he was married, she would never have let him in the house and that she never wanted to see him again. This very public humiliation at least gave me some comfort. As did the fact that he now had to take on an additional bank loan to pay for the new car. As for the old one, it was eventually restored with a new roof, windscreen and wing and given to my mother's old friend Peter.

Vladimir's drinking was getting worse. He had lost his job in the forestry works before and now was sacked again for being drunk and getting in a fight. He was unable to find a job elsewhere and although I tried to find a part time job as a cleaner these vacancies always seemed to be filled by younger girls with shorter skirts. Without his money we were struggling, with just my business income and the small amount of child allowance I was receiving from the state. It was a particularly hard winter that year with deep snow on the ground for months and good quality footwear was hard to find. We seemed to get through boots for the three children on a monthly basis. We bought a new pair for Olga one month, next month for Vita and the month after that for Vitaly and then it was back to Olga again. Fortunately, another source of income was soon to come my way. One day I had a call from Liana to say that her husband was looking for new staff. I should now explain that his business was a licenced brothel and he was short of two girls at the present time. When I was first told about this I was deeply shocked as I had no idea such things were legal in Germany as they certainly were not in Latvia. I also felt misgivings on a moral basis but I eventually understood that it was a business like any other as far as rules and regulations were concerned and the girls were probably better protected in a legal environment rather than working on their own if that was their chosen profession. Liana suggested a couple of likely candidates who she used to go to school with. I was asked to approach them to see if they were interested. Both had a child each but no husband so the solution was simple. They would go to Germany to work in the brothel and I would look after their children, who were about three years old. I would be paid by their mothers from their wages. They were already enrolled at the kindergarten, where after a while one of the staff came up to me one day and complimented me on how the children had changed since I had been looking after them. They were clean, smelt nice and behaved much better than before. After about six months I had managed to save something from the money sent to me, which mysteriously arrived in US dollars.

However, Vladimir still had not found a job and Liana, realising how serious it was becoming telephoned to say that she had found him a job in Bremen, herding cows. The job would be to let them out into the field after milking, clean out the sheds and herd them back in for the night. He took the job but it only lasted a month before he was sacked for being drunk on the job.

Instead of coming home, he made his way to Liana's flat in a state of drunkenness. Her husband, keen to help out, kindly gave him a job as a cleaner/caretaker at the brothel and initially, he was a great success. He was popular with the twenty or so girls who worked there and they gave him the nickname 'Putin' because of his resemblance to the Russian leader. His boss was equally pleased with him because he proved to be an excellent cleaner. The ground floor of the brothel was divided into rooms where the girls would entertain their clients and he lived in a room on first floor. This was also where the girls had their own rooms, some of them sharing. Once again, despite the good start, his downfall was drink. One of his duties was to keep the stocks of drink in the clients' rooms topped up, so he was entrusted with the key to the stockroom where he had access to all the different drinks on offer and could help himself to small amounts from bottles that were already opened without anyone being the wiser. It was like giving a small child the keys to a sweetshop, or as the Russian saying has it, letting the goat into the garden where the cabbages grow. As time passed, he would make frequent visits to this room and his increasing and obvious drunkenness of course did not go unnoticed. He received verbal warnings about his behaviour and his boss was very conscious of our situation back home, ensuring that his wages were being sent direct to my account in Madona, so he cut Vladimir a lot of slack before he was finally left with no choice. When Vladimir was sober he was a model of faithfulness but when drunk, another Vladimir took over who was a different character. The combination of scantily clad young girls and the drink must have been too strong a brew for him and on more than one occasion he would knock on the door of one of these girls only to be told to go away. To his credit, he was not so stupid as to try it on with one of the girls from Madona, but one day when they were off work, they invited him in for a drink. Bear in mind the girls worked till late at night, so the mornings were for sleeping, but in he went, to the room which they shared. The noise from their partying and the loud music was not appreciated by the girl in the next room who promptly told the boss. He contacted Liana before doing anything and she immediately came to the brothel, where together they went to the room in question, knocked on the door and on trying to open the door, found the key was in the lock inside. They got one of the girls to then try to get in by asking for a favour and the door was opened. The two girls were there, but no sign of Vladimir. Liana pulled back the duvets, nothing there. Then she looked under one of the beds and there he was, laying on the floor. She dragged him out by the legs, revealing a drunken, happy Vladimir with his erect member hanging out of his trousers. He was taken back to the flat, told he was sacked and given enough petty cash to buy himself a sandwich on his way back to Madona.

CHAPTER 16

Back home, in Vladimir's absence, peace and quiet reigned and the children and I were happy enough living a life without stress. He was a happy drunk but when sober was difficult to live with, being dictatorial and aggressive. He had had an unhappy childhood with a father who beat him almost daily for the most trivial reasons. He was always in trouble. If he had difficulty with his homework no one had any patience with him and he was often made to stand in the corner while the rest of the family had their evening meal and watched television. This would go on past midnight when he was finally allowed to go to bed. Such cruel behaviour to a young child no doubt had its effect on him and he tried to emulate his father in the way he treated the children and me. Thus it was a relief to be free of him for a few months while he was working in Germany.

The downside of this was that the duties he was usually responsible for fell on me. Our water supply was a deep well of spring water and this necessitated several visits a day, a large and heavy full bucket in each hand to be carried from the well to our kitchen. Some while before one morning Vladimir discovered a dead cat in the well. How it had got there was a mystery as the well was covered to prevent such accidents. No one from the local authority or a tradesman was interested in retrieving it or cleaning the well so between us we set about it and emptied the dirty water, cleaned up the sides of the well and buried the cat. The best that can be said of the well was that at least the water was free, but I would happily have traded that benefit for running water in a tap in the house. After the water there was then the firewood which had to be chopped up and taken from the woodshed to the house, and sundry other labour intensive tasks.

I was already suffering from back pains and a troublesome hip. A visit to the doctor confirmed that my hip was badly in need of replacement. It was possible to have this done free of charge but there was a waiting list of about a year. I was once confined to bed for a week unable to move with the pain and the doctor prescribed a self injection drug which I became dependent on to ease the pain.

In view of what had happened in Germany I was no longer interested in fostering the two children of the women who had been involved in Vladimir's escapade. It was still a shock that one day when I went to collect them from the kindergarten as usual I was told that another person had already come for them. It did not take long for the children to revert to their old habits under their new guardians as I was told by one of the supervisors subsequently that they were once again dirty, smelly and badly clothed. I was saddened to hear this and my last month's income from their mothers never materialised either.

On Vladimir's return I wanted a divorce. I had simply had enough of his constant misdemeanours and irresponsible behaviour. Against this, the reality of my situation was this. I was not in good health, my clothes business, like the Latvian economy generally, had declined to a trickle of what it was, as with the closure of so many factories and businesses following independence, so many people lost their jobs and most of my customers were struggling to get by and had no money for clothes. It was hardly worth my while to make my weekly trips to the wholesalers in Riga as I was barely covering the cost of the petrol to get there and back. In addition, we had loans for the car, a fridge and television which had to be serviced, so going forward on my own was not a realistic proposition. Vladimir did eventually manage to get his old job back in the forest, but his drinking was getting worse and there was never a day when he was sober. Living in the bungalow was simply too much to cope with so we decided to downsize to a flat. Having put the property up for sale I was surprised at how many people were interested and realised we had underpriced it. This was adjusted and very soon a woman with a two bedroom flat showed an interest in buying it so we came to an arrangement to swap properties with a cash adjustment on our favour. As she wanted to carry out some work on the bungalow before moving in we found temporary accommodation in a vacant three bed apartment. The problem was that we still had our two dogs, Tom and Dika. I managed to find a home for Dika quite easily but Tom, a very large German Shepherd dog, no one wanted. Tom was an outdoor dog, unused to living indoors and was not house trained. He took every opportunity to leave his calling card about the flat, and there were always puddles to clear up. He was also badly flea ridden. At the end of my tether and bearing in mind we were only tenants in a very temporary situation and with the flat stinking as a result of Tom's activities, desperate measures were called for. I bundled the children and Tom into the car (he was always very keen to be the first to jump in if we were going anywhere and was entirely oblivious of his fate) and we drove out to a remote village, down a farm track, dumped him in a cow shed and drove home. The children were upset, particularly Vitaly who loved Tom and was heartbroken. I was not proud of my actions either but a little while later, during the course of a conversation with a woman who lived in that area I found out that Tom had acquired new owners on the farm and all was well. Of course, I told her that the dog had ran away from us while we were out walking with him!

We then had a stroke of good luck as a three bedroomed flat became available to buy, which we negotiated in the usual way I have described before. It was in a bad way and we had to spend some money on repairs and redecorations but at last I had a bathroom, a luxury unknown previously. Within a few days of moving in I had the call for my hip operation. It had taken almost a year to the day. Although there was a well equipped hospital in Madona I had to go to a town called Valmeira for the operation. It was a good three hours and a half drive which made it very difficult for any members of my family to visit while I was there, and it proved to be even worse than I had feared. During my wait for the operation my hip had degenerated to the extent that my right leg was some 20 centimetres shorter than the left and walking was very difficult and I had a permanent limp. The morning after my arrival that afternoon I was wheeled into the operating theatre to be greeted by a surgeon I had never seen before and who knew nothing about my case other than the operation he was about to perform. I was given an injection in my lower back and the whole area around became numb and I started to drift off to sleep, only for the nurse to shake me awake. The surgeon then told her to let me sleep, but I remember being semi conscious and hearing the sound of a drill or a saw buzzing away. I never knew whether they had given me the correct anaesthetic or not but something did not seem right. I woke up in a different room to the one I had been in before the operation and was there for a couple of days. I later discovered that I had suffered an attack of tachycardia during the operation and was being kept under observation as a result. I spent most of the time asleep. Later I was moved back to the ward but never received any attention from medical staff at all. The only person I spoke to was the woman who brought me food. There were no toilet arrangements or any attention whatsoever.

I was feeling unwell and was convinced I had a high temperature so when Liana phoned me from Germany I told her about my lack of attention and how bad I felt. She subsequently got on to the hospital and shortly afterwards I was at last treated. I was indeed running a high temperature of over 40 degrees and had difficulty when I tried to stand up while they changed my bandages. As they removed the old dressing, about two litres of blood spurted out onto the bed. Very weak still, I had a job to stand up although that is a necessary part of the recovery from such an operation, and I was told I would need a further 14 days in hospital to recover. I was now thoroughly unhappy with the hospital and wanted to go home, so I had a very acrimonious conversation with the administrator about their shortcomings and it was arranged that Vladimir would pick me up in the VW Passat and take me home. I was situated on the fourth floor of the hospital and even taking the lift down to the ground floor was a trial. Vladimir, who had brought a crutch for me to lean on, had to all but carry me to the car and I laid down on the back seat for the journey home, feeling every little bump in the road. When we finally got back to the flat, there was one more challenge, climbing the two flights of stairs up to our front door. Finally, I made it and I had never felt so relieved to be home in my own bed that even though I was in pain and exhausted, I slept very soundly that night.   I was left with very bad impressions of that hospital and would never want to go back there but in accordance with Latvian custom to reward someone (even if you have paid for the service, or if it is free) and to my later regret, I made a present of $300 to the surgeon.

Olga left school at 16 and showed no signs of looking for work or wanting to go on to university, although she had left with good academic results. This became a source of irritation, as she would dress up in the evening, go out who knows where, and only return in the early hours of the morning. She would then go to bed and wake up in the middle of the afternoon and spent hours making herself up before going out again. Vladimir had managed to get himself sacked once again for the usual reasons but was now working at a wood processing plant, getting up at 5am to start work at 6, getting home in the early afternoon depending on how busy they were.   He was becoming increasingly exasperated with her behaviour and one day on getting home as she was rising from her slumbers he suggested that she could work at his plant where there was a clerical vacancy. She was not interested in this and a heated row soon developed at the end of which he slapped her face hard. This prompted her to pack her things and leave and we later heard that she had gone to Riga and was living in a flat there with a boyfriend. Of course I had a big row with Vladimir and told him that if he ever laid a finger on one of my children again, it would be he who would be packing his bags. I could of course sympathise with his point of view as he was working hard to keep a roof over our heads and she was contributing nothing, but the way he approached it in typical bull headed fashion was completely wrong.

A year later Vita left school as well and moved to Riga to be with her sister. She had been an exceptional athlete at school, but having suffered a number of injuries gradually wound down her involvement. Thus, we were now just the three of us.

CHAPTER 17

Olga and Vita used to visit us occasionally for birthdays and other special days but the atmosphere with Vladimir was strained beyond repair because of past events. As for Vitaly, who was now nearly a teenager, like so many children of his age, he tended to spend most of his leisure time in his bedroom playing on his computer or watching television or a video. I was always urging him to go out and get some exercise but like all his school mates, he wasn't interested in the outdoors. I suppose it was partly my fault for buying him all the things that enabled this unhealthy life style. I remember buying him the computer with a loan, and probably the television as well. The local economy had started to pick up, people had more money in their pockets and my clothes business which had virtually ceased, was revived to the extent that it soon outgrew its previous success. When we bought the flat we also acquired a garage which we rented. We did not use it to house the car, because it was no ordinary garage, being tall enough to enable a false ceiling to be installed, giving us storage space for things like a sledge, skis and bits of furniture we were not using at the time. At 'ground level' we had a sofa, table and chairs and often had barbecues there and this made up for the lack of a garden and the outside space we had been used to in the bungalow.

Vladimir was still working at the wood processing plant and still getting drunk regularly, often phoning me to take him home as he was incapable of walking. One day, for a change, he was not drunk just extremely tired. The factory had a high turnover of staff and some new people, including women, had been recruited and training them was hard work, as well as slowing down production and thus extending their hours. It happened that as well as Vladimir I also gave a lift to one of his workmates, who told me there was a new woman who had started there whose eyes were constantly on my husband and I had better watch out.

It was now winter and the weather was icy cold as only a Latvian winter can be and one night Vladimir did not come home at the usual time. After a while I drove to the works but finding it in darkness and obviously closed, drove home. There was nothing more to be done but at about four in the morning, there was a knocking at the door and it was Vladimir as drunk as could be. He staggered to bed and woke up a couple of hours later just as drunk as when he had gone to bed in order to go to work. That night he again failed to come home but then it was the weekend, which passed without incident.

On Monday he went to work at about half past five as usual but I was woken up by a phone ringing about six thirty. I got up to answer it but it was his phone that was ringing, he must have forgotten to

144

take it with him to work and was probably ringing me to ask me to drop it off for him. However, I did not recognise the number so when I answered it, I said nothing. A woman's voice began speaking saying that she understood why he couldn't speak and that she really wanted to see him again at the same place as before. A short 'who are you?', 'who are you?' dialogue took place. I then put the phone down and used my phone to call her back. 'Vladimir was a wonderful man and a great lover and why is he with such an old woman' were just some of the things said to me, as well as graphic details of sex on the workroom floor among the sawdust. I told her she was welcome to take him any time she liked and he could go to her with my blessing.

I thought about what to do next and decided to go to the factory and give him his phone. When I saw him I told him that I knew everything that he had been up to and I wanted him to leave. I had only been home about twenty minutes when he turned up. Of course, he had his excuses ready. They had had a lot to drink at work, this woman especially had drunk much too much and there was no one else to see her home safely, so he had to and what happened afterwards was the result of the drink and didn't mean anything. He than phoned her and told her that there was no way he would live with her, that she was a terrible mother to her seven year old son, that it had all been a big mistake and he would never leave me. Even if I left him, we would never go with her. He went back to work and came home sober but things had gone too far this time. I no longer loved him and could not put up with his behaviour any longer.

A few days later he failed to come home one Friday night. By now I had given up on him and ceased to care where he was or with whom after what had happened so many times. It was a bitterly cold night, the icicles were foot long needles hanging from the guttering outside the flat, the snow was deep, temperature double degrees below freezing and it was raining on an already icy surface. Next morning, one of our neighbours in the flat next door went downstairs to take her dog for a walk and on opening the front door of the block, was confronted by the sight of Vladimir, laying flat on his back in a puddle of water, out cold. She knocked on my door, and fearing the worst, I rushed downstairs with Vitaly to see if he was still alive.

He was icy cold to touch but breathing and still very drunk. Between us we hauled him up the two flights of stairs and dragged him into the flat by his boots. We managed to take his dirty, sodden clothes off, clean him up and cover him with three duvets, after applying the magic potion that Latvians swear by, vodka spirit. Miraculously, considering his night out laying in water on a bed of ice, he was not at all ill and was able to go to work on Monday as if nothing had happened. The

146

episode reminded me of something that had happened years before when I was coming home with Pavel from my mother's and we saw a man we recognised lying in the middle of the road in similar wintry conditions and just as drunk. I went to his wife's address to tell her but her attitude was 'let him freeze to death for all I care' and slammed the door in my face. We tried to lay him on the pavement but for some reason he kept crawling back to the road and in the end we had to leave him. We found out later that he had died of hypothermia and his wife, too late in the day, was full of remorse for her lack of help.

Predictably, Vladimir lost his job soon after. His boss explained to me that he had been given one last chance after another but he could not go on employing someone so completely unreliable. At this point Vladimir admitted he had a problem and I booked him in to a clinic where they would try to dry him out. This was some distance away from Madona and during the long drive, he was of course drunk. We had a consultation with the doctor and we had to give our written consent to his planned treatment. After a week, I was called to go the clinic to take him home. We were both told that he had been given certain injections that if he took so much as a tiny drop of alcohol, it would prove fatal. We had to sign a disclaimer that if he did take alcohol within a year, the hospital would not be responsible for the consequences. I have no way of knowing if all they told us was true, nor what exactly the injections were, but we believed them. He had to carry a card in his wallet to warn against being administered any drugs containing alcohol in the event of an accident.

For nine months he never touched a drop, probably the longest period in his life he had managed to abstain. His temper was not improved by his abstinence unfortunately and there was one particular incident that stands out in my memory. He and Vitaly were watching television while I was preparing some soup, which I brought in and placed on the table next to them. Vitaly was at the age where boys cannot keep still, his feet were twitching and he was wriggling about, so much so that he knocked the bowl of soup flying, all over Vladimir, the sofa and the floor. Vladimir jumped up in a rage and began to rain blows on him and I intervened to stop him as he was so furious he might have killed him. Vladimir had been prescribed tablets in case the stress of his no alcohol regime became too much, but he refused to take them.

In the course of my clothing business, I often was presented with boxes of confectionary from appreciative customers, and one such was a box of liqueur chocolates. I noticed one day that they were gradually disappearing and became suspicious as I had not eaten any and nor had Vitaly. One day, I happened to glance out of my bedroom window and saw Vladimir staggering across the road, going in the general direction if his parents' flat. After a while I telephoned his mother to enquire if he was there. He was of course, and she was very protective of him, saying he was only a little bit drunk and would be sleeping there that night.

He had managed to get another job after being discharged from the clinic as the driver of a shop on wheels, with a woman I knew, selling goods in the villages around Madona. This lasted about a year until he found a better paid job as a driver, picking up consignments of food from the wholesaler and delivering them to various supermarkets and smaller shops in the villages over quite a wide area. The stock control was very lax and he often had leftovers from the delivery schedule. At first, he attempted to return them to the depot, but the other drivers soon put him right on that as it was common practice for them to keep surplus items for themselves. As well as this, quite often the boss used to give to the drivers a variety of food that was unaccounted for. So it was that our freezer was always well stocked with vast quantities of food, ensuring we never went hungry.

One day I got a call from him to say that he would be home in forty minutes but I could tell by his voice that he was already a bit tipsy. He was surprised that I could tell but I knew him very well by now. He had only had one glass of brandy but by the time he got home he would be in a bad way of course. He had started to use a lot of chewing gum to disguise the smell of alcohol on his breath and had almost inevitably slipped back into his old ways.

He was given an assignment for some weeks driving to Riga every evening, leaving home at about ten o'clock to get to a meat processing plant and load their products in order to deliver them to different locations the next day, getting home in the early afternoon. I went with him a couple of times and could see that it was very hard work, with a couple of hours free to grab some sleep in the cab. He did not drink when I was with him, but alone it was a different story. He became friendly with a woman at the plant who helped him load the lorry and the other drivers became resentful of his behaviour, drinking and entertaining her in his cab. This woman even took to phoning him at home so that on one occasion I spoke to her and told her I was going to visit her husband in Riga and let him know what she doing. Vladimir of course protested that they were only drinking together but we had been there before and I was weary of his excuses, so much so that I packed his belongings in two suitcases and dropped them off at his mothers, told him I wanted him out of my life and blocked his number on by phone. For four or five days I withdrew from the world, shutting myself away in my bedroom and not eating or drinking anything as

I just wanted to curl up and die. Eventually, through a well meaning friend of a friend, I had a phone call from an unattached man in Riga, who looked after his sick mother. We got talking and decided to meet. I drove to Riga for the weekend and we booked into a hotel and had an idyllic weekend, enjoying long walks and pleasant conversations and nice food in the hotel restaurant. As ever, Vladimir found a way to spoil things. Having blocked him from my phone, he bought a new one and the last night in the hotel my phone rang at four in the morning. My new companion answered it, to Vladimir's surprise and they had a long conversation in which my husband was told a few home truths. When I got back home, he was waiting in the hallway begging to be taken back and pledging to be a reformed character. After a few weeks of constant harassment I relented but this time it was purely for economic reasons. Life would be impossible without his wages and I was trapped. As for the other man, I never saw him again but I will always remember that weekend with affection.

As I have said, Vladimir's exploits at the meat processing plant had already upset the other drivers and word of his disruptive behaviour got back to his boss and he was given a new schedule. This involved driving to Gulbene, a much shorter journey with less scope for misadventure, at least in theory. On the third day of his new route, I received an incoherent phone call from him. Drunk as ever, he had been stopped by the police, taken out of the cab and his keys confiscated. They telephoned his boss who duly drove there and picked him up and also had to send another man to drive the lorry back to the depot. My heart sank as this would surely end in the sack, but his remarkably tolerant boss gave him another chance. This time, he would simply be responsible for loading and unloading while somebody else took the wheel. Sadly, this act of charity was repaid by yet more trouble. His behaviour in the cab, drunken and argumentative, soon led to the driver refusing to work with him and his replacement soon came to the same conclusion. Still his boss took pity on him and reassigned him to merely loading duties at the depot. When the court case came up and Valdimir was banned from driving for two years and fined 700 Euros, his boss even paid his fine, taking a small amount out of his wages each week in repayment. He was very lucky to have such a benevolent employer, who seemed to have the patience of a saint in the face of his continual misdemeanours.

When Vladimir returned home after the incident with the police he was in a an extremely angry and aggressive mood. We had a big row. I told him his behaviour had completely ruined his reputation in our small town where everybody knew your own business before you did and I felt ashamed to be associated with him. I felt sure he was going to get sacked and how would we pay the bills as my clothing business was once again going through a quiet time with many of my customers on hard times and an ever increasing number paying me by instalments rather than upfront. He had let his family down once again. At this he exploded and going to our large freezer, started grabbing food from it and hurling it at me, all the while declaring that this is what he was doing for the family, feeding us with his hard work etc. I was bombarded with all manner of sausages, frozen chicken, joints of meat and anything else he could get his hands on. It was a warm day, and the windows were open. Vitaly was outside with a friend and heard the commotion coming from our flat. Greatly alarmed and fearing for my safety, he phoned the police, who arrived in about two minutes to witness a scene of complete carnage with food all over the place and Vladimir still in a towering rage. The upshot was they frogmarched him away to the police station and his parting shot to Vitaly was 'I shall never forgive you for this' as they took him away to spend a night in the cells. Vitaly helped me put the food back in the freezer and it was then I realised how badly bruised I was by the assault. I had bumps on my head, swollen lips and my arms were covered in bruises. All in all it took about a week for me to recover. When we were cleaning the flat later that week, I moved the sofa to clean under it and discovered something that looked like a cat's droppings.   It turned out to be a small sausage from the fracas that had gone bad.

After this incident I was desperate to get away and start a new life.   Vladimir's endless cycle of drunkenness resulting in so many disastrous outcomes had become just too much to bear. I was in fairly regular telephone contact with a Latvian woman who lived in Ireland who I had known for many years. She worked on a mushroom farm in County Mayo where there were vacancies and she had a house with a spare room where she could put me up.   Without knowing any more, this seemed to be too good an opportunity to miss if I really was serious about escaping from the traumas of life with Vladimir. My only concern was Vitaly, as I did not feel able to leave him alone with his father. The solution came in the form of Marija, my father's sister, who kindly agreed to move into our flat in my absence and act as housekeeper. I bought a ticket to Dublin and flew to what I hoped would be the start of a new life in Ireland.

CHAPTER 18

It was Autumn 2008 when I set foot on Irish soil at Dublin airport. Ruta had sent someone to pick me up and I was driven to our destination, a small village consisting of a few houses, a food store, a post office and pub. Ruta and her husband had a large detached house where one room was already occupied by a man from Latvia who worked on the farm and I was given a room with a bed and a cupboard. I had brought just a suitcase with my minimal and very basic belongings.

The next day we went to the mushroom farm and I was quickly taken on as a picker and the basic requirements of the job explained to me. I had to pick, weigh and pack the mushrooms to various specifications and my hours were 7am to 7pm with three 15 minute breaks, only time enough for a quick snack and a visit to the toilet. It was a large farm with many workers, mostly from Eastern European countries and Latvians, Poles, Ukrainians and other nationalities all naturally formed their own little cliques based on their country of origin. There was a lot of friendliness to your face but gossip behind your back. It was also very tiring work for long hours but relatively well paid, especially in relation to wages in our native countries, producing about 600 Euros a week. As winter approached, it seemed to rain incessantly every day and the routine of long hours and getting home tired and having to cook a meal in the large kitchen which was shared by all of us, was starting to take its toll. To make matters worse, it was turning cold and there was no heating in my room. I had to pay Ruta for my accommodation of course but also for my share of the electricity bill, which seemed a bit unfair as I only had one light in the room and I noticed one day when her bedroom door was open, that Ruta had a large radiator! I send money back home once a month. No computer, no local bank so I had no option but to send cash in an envelope. Ruta advised me to split the money I was ending, about 400 Euros, into four different envelopes which is just as well I did, because one of those I sent in the first month never arrived. The money was of course sent to Marija, but Vladimir was as usual up to his old tricks, offering to do the shopping for my aunt and then treating himself to drinks with the money left over after he had bought all the items on her shopping list. Later, ironically, he lost his job, not through any escapade of his own this time but because the company went out of business and he was made redundant. He was given unemployment benefit which was to last 12 months, so in typical fashion, spent his time lying on the sofa, sleeping in front of the television and drinking.

During this time of increasing disillusionment I was in touch with my daughters. Liana was happy enough in Germany and Olga and Vita now had different lives. Olga had moved to Riga some years before as I mentioned, but the man she was with got involved in drug dealing and she left him. Later, working in a bar in Riga she met an Englishman named Alan, who had business interests in Latvia and became friendly with him. Later, she went to England to be with him and they married. Vita meanwhile had a boyfriend named Alexander who had a friend in Ireland. This friend got a job for Alexander and they moved there on the strength of it. It was not near where I worked, so I never saw her while I was in Ireland. They all advised me that the best thing to do was to go back home to Latvia. In any case, the farm was starting to go through hard times (it would eventually go bust) and my hours were cut.

So I decided to go home. I took a train to Dublin and remember feeling a sense of relief that I was leaving what had increasingly become a nightmare and I never thought I would be so looking forward to seeing my homeland again. Vladimir had been pleading with me to come home for some time and was at the bus station to meet me with a bouquet of roses. We got home and Marija very tactfully left to go back to her flat, leaving me, Vladimir and Vitaly to be together. I opened the fridge, of course it was empty so we had to get some food in. As I was producing a 100 Euro note from my wallet, Vladimir asked how much I had brought back with me. I will never forget his response when I told him

3000 Euros. "Only 3000?" Only! Despite this, I was glad to be home and to see that Vitaly seemed well enough. As to the future, I was echoing the thoughts of one of my favourite fictional heroines, Scarlett O'Hara, when I mused 'After all, tomorrow is another day'.

CHAPTER 19

My euphoria at being back home soon evaporated.
Nothing had changed. Vladimir was out of work
with his benefits ended. The 3000 Euros I had
brought back soon were whittled away and the bills
as ever had to be paid and once again things were
looking desperate.
I could not find any work and my age was starting
to go against me. There was a man who
transported goods and people from Latvia to
England who would have taken us on his bus with a
promise to find us a job there in exchange for 300
Euros but at 50 I was ruled out as too old. I
chanced to meet someone in town who told me that
jobs were plentiful in the Czech Republic. This
sounded promising and he gave me a phone
number which would put me in touch with someone
who could help. After sending our CVs as
requested we were given instructions as to what to
do next. Marija came to our rescue again by
agreeing to move back to our flat and look after
Vitaly.
We were to be picked up by a private bus and
driven to the Czech Republic. There were about
thirty of us in all. I don't recall exactly when I
started to have my suspicions that this new
adventure might not be a good idea but perhaps it
was when we stopped under a bridge in the Prague
area and a man who announced himself as our

boss asked for our passports to be handed over. He examined each one carefully and when he got to mine said I was too old. However as Vladimir was younger they would take me on probation to see if I was employable. His manner was severe and bullying and he had a way of making people feel intimidated. He was not a Czech, and I later found out he was from Chechnya. We were than herded into a building which to call it a hotel would be far fetched, but this was to be our home for the foreseeable future. We were shown into a room which contained one wardrobe, a table and five single beds. There was me, Vladimir and a couple with their twenty something son and we were to share this room with them all the time we were there. The only facility for cooking was a hot plate in the corridor and this was shared by all the inmates. There were two toilets and a shower room and they were all in a disgusting state but we had no choice. There were always queues for both and I used to get up at four in the morning before anyone else so that I could cook a breakfast for us. One morning when I brought Vladimir his breakfast in bed the woman with whom we shared the room asked me why I was doing this when he couldn't even be bothered to thank me? Was he a king or something?

As far as the jobs were concerned, we had a journey of about an hour to get to the factory where we were employed, first a train journey then a bus, all at our own expense. Our working hours were six in the morning until six at night. We had begun to realise that we were not directly employed by the factory but by the Chechen gangmaster who had engaged us and we were treated like dirt by the Czech workers in the factory. To them we were barely human beings and every word to us was spat out with contempt. This was indeed modern day slavery.

Vladimir was employed as a   fork lift driver, something which he was well experienced in and he was highly thought of, and to his credit, not drinking. My job was in the packing department where we had to work with assembling cardboard cartons and boxes and then filling them with cosmetics, soaps, perfumes etc. Within a short time, the often sharp edges of the cardboard had cut and chafed my fingers and at night the throbbing from the pain would often keep me awake. A supervisor kept account of the number of boxes we packed and the list would vary from time to time. There was one occasion where we were packing washing powders in their bags into boxes. The bags were 15 kilos in weight and lifting those into the boxes once they had been assembled was an arduous task. After one such bag was in the box, I closed the lid perhaps too emphatically and a great cloud of powder exploded in my face from the bag, which could not have been properly closed. For a few days my face was badly marked by the results of whatever chemical the powder contained, penetrating my skin and being very painful.

One day a woman queried the fact that she had been underpaid when she received her wage packet. For this temerity she beaten up by one of the thugs who worked for the Chechen gangmaster and the assault took place in front of us all, thus having the intimidating effect required and keeping the increasingly cowed workforce in line. Vladimir was well paid for his job, receiving 25000 Crowns per month, which was probably around 1000 Euros a month then but I only had 15000. The first month I was 5000 short and I queried this with the man giving out the wage packets. I went back to my room and he soon followed, threatening me for daring to raise the matter in front of the other workers. It was a mistake which would be rectified tomorrow, he said. Funny that it was a mistake that had been made in their favour, not in mine, I rejoined. The difference was indeed made up the following day but I was fearful that I had stepped out of line and what the consequences might be.

Conditions were becoming unbearable in every respect. A horrible job, dreadful, cramped and often insanitary living conditions (the toilets never seemed to be cleaned and were often blocked with excrement or vomit or both) with no privacy in our room which we shared. Washing was difficult as the shower was always in use and having to wash your clothes in the shower because there was nowhere else was difficult with the result that the clothes we wore became dirty and smelly. To make matters worse, Vladimir had started drinking again and this was noticed by his bosses.. I needed a break and following a Skype call from Olga, it was arranged that I would fly to England to spend a week with her and Alan. Unpaid leave of course. It was my first time in England and I loved it. It was different from anything I had ever known and when the time came for me to go home I was heartbroken. Eight months as a virtual slave was more than enough. I went back to work with a heavy heart but Olga promised to look out for a job for me in England and as Christmas was near I could spend it with them. I told Vladimir about this but no else, so it was that at 4am one morning I crept quietly out of the room with my suitcase and escaped from this life of slavery before anyone knew I was gone.

CHAPTER 20

We had a lovely Christmas and New Year and the relief I felt at my escape from my Czech hellhole was beyond words, but as the New Year of 2010 began, I had to think about the future. I had been taught English at school, but that was many years ago and not much of it had stuck, but being with Olga and Alan for a while helped me to acquire some ability to understand the language and to tentatively try to speak it. I started to write down so many words a day, and everyday expressions as well, to gradually build up my vocabulary and I also bought a textbook of useful words and phrases which never left my side and which I would go to sleep trying to memorise.

Olga was looking for a job for me and as it happened there was an agency in Bognor Regis, where there was a sizeable East European, mainly Polish minority, who specialised in recruiting workers for the many market gardening and fruit and vegetable packing jobs that were available in the area. She also found me a room to rent in the town and I was taken on by the agency. My first job in England was to pick seedlings and box them at a market gardening site. It was a job that kept me on my feet for 12 hours a day working in a large greenhouse with about fifteen other people, mainly from Poland and the Baltic countries with just a few English people. The work was for twelve hours, five days a week and we were given two fifteen minute breaks and one for half an hour. After deductions, I took home about £250 a week, which was good money to me, but probably derisory to a British person.

In the meantime, Vladimir was anxious to join me in England and after my first few weeks wages were received and I had paid the rent, I bought him a ticket to fly to England from Prague. My Aunt Marija had been receiving his money back in Madona to pay for the bills and Vitaly's upkeep etc so now he needed to find a job. He worked for a while in a nursery greenhouse but in the autumn, much to my surprise, as I had not thought of England as a wine producing country, he got a job grape picking some distance away in the Sussex countryside. He was ferried to and fro by workmates who had a car. Needless to say, most of that workforce was from our part of the world. After the season was over, he went back to the greenhouse work.

Our living conditions were far from ideal. We had to share a kitchen and toilets with four other households in the building but at least we both had work and compared to our previous existence life was so much better.

The agency offered me a change of job at a large nursery specialising in herbs, watercress and salads and I began working there, initially on a production line weighing the produce which would then be sorted out for quality and assigned to various well known supermarkets and food stores.

I took my book with me and found space for it on my table near the scales and was intent on picking up what my supervisor, who was English, had to say. She was a very helpful, patient lady named Maria, who encouraged me and made a point after a few weeks, of telling me how much my English had improved. On occasion I would be called into her office to act as an interpreter when she had trouble explaining something to one of the workers. After a couple of months I was called into her office and told I was being offered a contract to be an employee of the company rather than continue as agency staff. I was asked to read the contract through and sign it, but I was stuck on one point which I did not understand. It turned out this was a clause agreeing that I would not cough, sneeze or blow my nose when in the vicinity of the produce. I was of course delighted with the news and felt I had arrived at last. I began to work on a shift pattern of 6am-2pm one week with 2pm-10pm the following.

At home, we made arrangements to move to rented accommodation in an end of terrace house where we would have an upstairs room and the usual shared kitchen and toilet. At first it seemed an improvement but it tuned out worse. We were sharing with three other occupants. One of them was an Estonian woman who was prone to steal our food from the communal kitchen. One day when I was at work, she helped herself to some salad which I had prepared and left covered on the kitchen table. She suffered from hepatitis and to make matters worse, had used the spoon I had left in the salad. I told her that she was welcome to our food if she was that desperate, but did not appreciate her thieving nor the lack of hygiene.

Back in Madona, Vitaly had finished school and we were anxious for him to come to England but accommodation was a problem. We were not supposed to have anyone else in our room and it was not ideal anyway, but he joined us, sometimes sleeping on the sofa in the television room shared by all. This did not go down well with the other tenants who threatened to report us to the landlord. We could not continue like this but fortunately, he was offered a bed at Olga and Alan's flat. He stayed with them for about a year and a half, taking various jobs such as working in a recycling plant, a fish and chip shop, a burger bar and a pizza place.

Another problem was that our room was on the side of the building with an exposed outside wall where the mortar was in bad repair, with the result that rain got in and quite often wetted the bed next to the wall. It was not just us that had problems as one night we were woken by a noise from next door, The walls were paper thin and you could hear every little sound. I went out to the corridor and found the man from the next room in a state of agitation. Water was cascading through his ceiling onto his bed. He tried to contact the owner but there was no reply. In the end his girl friend came and drove him back to her place for the night.

That year tragedy struck Vladimir's family in the summer of 2011 when his sister, only 33, died of cancer. I arranged for him to fly back to Latvia for the funeral and drew out £500 so that he would be able to cover any expenses while there for the week. His mother, protective as ever, wondered why I had allowed her boy to fly there all by himself but I had no holiday due and could not take the time off work. The day of the funeral I telephoned to see how everyone was and a familiar story reappeared. Vladimir was very drunk, was dishing out paper money as if he was a lord and behaving very badly, especially on such a sad occasion. His mother's sister in particular was appalled by his behaviour and asked me how on earth I put up with him. After a week, I got a call from him that he was coming home and I arranged for him to be picked up from the airport. Fortunately, by this time I had a car, which I used to drive to and from work. When I got home that day I had a call from Vladimir's driver to say that he was in the middle of Bognor and could not get any sense out of Vladimir as to where he lived as he was dead drunk. I drove into town and picked him up and took him home. To cap it all, he had no money left to pay the driver and when he got home, crashed out in the middle of the bed, leaving no room for me to lie down when I wanted to go to sleep.

Although we were stuck with this situation for the time being, towards the end of the year our situation dramatically improved. Olga knew a man who owned a property to let near Brighton. This was a big house with the opportunity for all the family to be together, apart from Liana and Sergei of course. So it was, we all moved in there. Vladimir and myself, Olga and Alan and Vitaly. We were soon joined by Vita and Alexander, who came over from Ireland as well with a view to settling in England, but they had a big row and he went back to Ireland on his own, never to be seen again. Christmas 2011 was the first time we had all been together for a long while and at last everything seemed settled.

CHAPTER 21

For a time, everything, or nearly everything, was fine. I was happy in my job although I now had a long commute every day. For my early shift I had to rise at about 3.30am to wash and have breakfast, leaving at 4am to drive to Bognor. At about 5.15 I would arrive in the town and pick up four passengers who all worked at my place, which helped with their contributions towards the diesel, and we started work at 6am. Vitaly had been working at a recycling plant and managed to get his father a job there as well. Everything should have been all right.

The continual fly in the ointment was Vladimir. His behaviour when sober was always aggressive and challenging and he constantly locked horns with Vitaly, especially early in the morning. Vitaly wanted to be quiet and have his breakfast in peace and quiet but Vladimir was always goading him. Early one morning when I wasn't working and was still half asleep in bed, I heard a commotion from downstairs and went to see what the trouble was. Vladimir and Vitaly were fighting, and I had to step in between them and break it up. Vitaly ran out of the house to get away from any trouble, which meant a long wait for the work bus and had no food for the day. I told my husband that if he ever touched Vitaly again he would be sorry and many other things I had said before.

Our relationship was plumbing new depths, if that was possible after all that had happened. I was very happy at work but often had to work longer hours than my allotted shift. Sometimes this meant a fifteen hour day including the car journey and I arrived home exhausted. I would go to our room and find Vladimir slumped out in bed, drunk as usual with the room stinking of alcohol. One day in particular I got home after a particularly stressful day at work and a pig of a car journey home and just could not face going into the house. I sat in the car on the front drive and could not stop crying. It must have been about an hour before I could summon up enough energy to go inside, knowing what I was going to be faced with. I had felt cold all day at work as we were dealing with herbs that needed to be maintained at a low temperature in a refrigerated chamber which made things worse so all I wanted to do was to shower and have a good few hours sleep before having to rise at 4am to begin another long day. In a deep sleep I was suddenly shoved violently out of bed by Vladimir and landed on the floor where I lay shaking with fright for a good while before recovering my understanding of what had happened. Later I was told without a hint of remorse that he had quite deliberately pushed me out as hard as he could because my snoring was disturbing him.

Money was becoming an issue. We had always pooled our wages to pay for the bills and our food but he started to keep his wage packet to himself for some reason. He was plainly fed up with working at the recycling plant and aiming to get the sack because he started drinking in the morning before going to work, thus ensuring that he would be sent home. He had two warnings and after the third he was sacked, clearly what he wanted to happen so that he could devote himself to his full time occupation of drinking.

He then announced that he was very tired and wanted to go back to Latvia for a short time, and relax, going fishing, meeting old friends etc. He once again played on my hopes that one day he would change by promising that he would use this time wisely and keeping sober, would straighten himself out and come back refreshed and a changed man. After nearly 25 years of his broken promises I should have known better but I fell for it again and he was soon on his way back to Latvia with two bags of clothing and food and the keys to the flat.

My Aunt Marija used to check up on the flat a couple of times a week to make sure all was well and continued to do so. On the first of her visits since Vladimir had taken up residence she opened the door and could hardly see into the flat because of the clouds of smoke that greeted her. He was lounging on the sofa with another drinking buddy, smoking like a chimney and there were bottles everywhere. I also had a phone call from a woman in the neighbouring flat, the same person who had discovered Vladimir laying in the snow years before. She was worried that because of the heavy smoking going on that there was a risk of fire if the drunks went to sleep with their cigarettes still burning, which I quite understood. She also told me that when walking her dog she had looked up at a window and seen a number of people drinking and smoking and that there were a few women there, including one who had her arms round Vladimir, who seeing her down below, quickly ushered everyone away from the window.

Something had to be done and quickly. The next day I telephoned Vladimir and told him he had half an hour to pack his bags and get out of the flat, failing which I would get the police involved. He was always very brave with women but a coward in the face of male authority and put up no resistance. It so happened that Marija's daughter, Svetlana, was visiting her that week and I arranged for them to go to the flat. I also sorted out a locksmith to change the locks to coincide with their arrival. Vladimir must have phoned his mother because she arrived at the flat as well and helped him to pack up and go back to her place. It took Svetlana the rest of the day to clean up the mess he had made and restore the flat to its former condition. The day after I phoned him and told him he had three days to get his details removed from the property and register at his mother's. The sheer relief at finally getting him out of my life was immense. In the early years, as a woman with young children I felt they needed a father and to be fair to him, he was good to them during that time. I was always trying to keep the family together and gave him last chance after last chance in the vain hope that one day, growing older he might change. In the later years, although my daughters were grown up and led their own lives, my son Vitaly was still very young and I felt still needed a father. Vitaly was quite forthright on the subject however and urged me to divorce him as he was increasingly upset at the way I was being treated. Even when they were sharing things like playing games on the PlayStation, if Vladimir happened to lose he would lash out physically and verbally. He had no sense of humour and could not bear to lose. It was like heaven to come home after work to an atmosphere of peace and quiet, knowing that there was not going to be any trouble. As for Vladimir, I heard that he had got a job back in forestry. He was trying to obtain an HGV licence so I sent him money to help pay for the exam, which he failed eight times before passing at the ninth attempt. Remembering how he had been with the children when they were young, I sent him clothes that I bought in England for his work and various other items after which I felt any debt was fully discharged and I could finally put all those wasted years behind me.

CHAPTER 22

Almost from the moment I first set foot in England I had felt at home. It felt so comfortable and although I had only a smattering of the language I could sense a different kind of atmosphere between people. There were little things like road courtesy, where other drivers would acknowledge you if you let them out in front of you and pedestrians waved to thank you if you let them cross the road. Things like civility from the staff in shops and 'Good Mornings' from strangers on the street when you passed them by all gave me a sense of well being and belonging. It offered a stark contrast to the way people were in my own country, where it seemed everyone went round with a long face and the everyday niceties of human interaction were a rarity. I don't know if it's the harsh winter climate, the economic hardship so many Latvians endure or the history of a country ravaged by war and the plaything of larger powers that has all contributed to this and the analysis of national characteristics is beyond my pay grade, so all I can speak of is my own experiences and how that has made me a confirmed Anglophile. I can honestly say that I have never once experienced any xenophobic behaviour towards me and from the start I tried to assimilate the British way of life. Notwithstanding, there are some things that I have carried over from my upbringing and two of these are my love of flowers and as I have alluded to before, my abiding love of the forests of my homeland and harvesting wild mushrooms and fruits. These things feed my soul and while it is easy to buy flowers, or have them bought for me, the forests here are not the same and I sometimes yearn for them.

Now a free agent and with an enthusiasm for all things British, I decided to sign up to a dating site for mature people, hoping to meet someone for friendship in the first place, and I had a brief encounter with a very pleasant man who drove a double decker bus for a living. We used to go for walks together and the occasional meal out and this went on for a few months. In the summer of that year I was invited by Olga and Alan to go on holiday with them to Turkey. It was the first time in my life I had ever actually had a proper holiday. Other than visits to relatives I had never been away from it all and I loved it. Beautiful beaches, lovely food and a sense of well being made it a memorable ten days. When I got back, I didn't give my friend a thought but he contacted me after a while to see if I was back and I told him that I no longer wanted to see him. My next encounter ended before it began. I arranged to meet a man in Brighton to go for a coffee but when I saw him I knew immediately he was not for me and finished it there and then. From then on, I decided that I would put all my efforts into my work and fill my life up with the pleasures of retail therapy as close personal relationships seemed to be beyond my reach as I felt then. My resolve did not last long as, through the dating agency, I met an older man, probably in his mid seventies, who lived in Bognor. We got on well together and he suggested that I could stay at his bungalow to make my journey to work much shorter. This was very good from my point of view, but it soon became a problem when I had to get up early for my 6am shift as although I was as quiet as a mouse, it always disturbed him and he was someone who needed his sleep. I gradually spent less and less time with him and eventually ceased seeing him altogether. We had a very amicable and enjoyable time together in an entirely platonic relationship but there was no future in it.

Shortly after this a new man came into my life in the early part of 2015. I saw his profile on the dating site and he sounded interesting but there was one major obstacle. Although he was just turned 70, he had long hair and an unruly beard and moustache and the resemblance to Father Christmas was striking. This did not appeal to me at all. Despite this we started sending each other messages and arranged to meet. This was on a Saturday lunchtime in a supermarket car park where I almost ran him over as he was waiting for me. The first thing to clear up was that my internet name was a pseudonym and then for him to find out I was from

Latvia. We went to a nearby pub and had coffees and a long chat about many subjects and the end result was that we arranged to meet again. This was the following week and we met in the evening and had a couple of drinks, which was too much for me as I had a struggle to drive the short distance home. He was a retired bank manager who lived in a flat in Eastbourne. His wife had died of cancer some years before, since when he had been in a relationship with a woman which had recently ended.

Our next meeting was to be at his place. Because of a misunderstanding he drove to Peacehaven to pick me up while I set off in my car to Eastbourne and we exchanged messages on our phones which eventually resolved the matter, and I arrived at his flat at the same time as he got back!

We very soon realised that we were in love and started to plan our future together. The first thing we sorted out was his hair. He willingly went along with my suggestions of a new look and so we visited the barbers where he was shorn of the excess hair and in my opinion looked ten years younger. When I met some of his friends later they hardly recognised him. I was introduced to his two sisters, who were both older than him, and I was made to feel very welcome. It was a completely new experience for me to be treated with such warmth and love compared to my previous relationships and I felt a real sense of belonging.

There was no inquisition about my past, no awkward moments and I recall one time with special warmth. We became engaged in early April and he bought me a lovely ring. We were dining out with his younger sister and her husband when he made the announcement and I will never forget how she jumped up and put her arms around me and made me feel so accepted.

Before we met, he had sold his flat but was waiting for the buyers to arrange a date for completion as they were moving back to the UK from abroad and there was no hurry. He had been looking at a smaller place than his very spacious three bedroom flat but had not decided on anything. In the meantime, there was lots to sort out. I was still married to Vadimir and now was the time to get my divorce sorted out so that I could marry my new love. I flew back to Latvia and confronted him my request to agree to a divorce so that it could take place with the minimum of delay. He protested that he still loved me and wanted me back and things would be different in the future. I had to play clever here, as he was quite likely to refuse to agree and a contested petition could take ages to be concluded. I therefore told him that if he changed his ways over time and became a reformed character then I would not close the door on us getting back together and this was enough for him to sign the papers. Of course I had no such intention but it was the only way to get my freedom. I returned to England very happy that at last I had put the last 25 years behind me and could look forward to a new and brighter future.

CHAPTER 23

With my divorce sorted out we could make plans for our wedding and we arranged it for July. I had some time off work and stayed at Gerry's flat where I slept more soundly than I had for years. After a great deal of thought we decided it would be a good idea to move nearer my place of work if we could find somewhere suitable. I had no plans for giving up work which I enjoyed and the journey to and from Eastbourne was not viable so we settled on a three bed mid terraced house on the outskirts of Bognor, which was not ideal, but the best option we could find.

With the help of a mortgage broker, Gerry managed to get the necessary finance teed up and we were all set to move there one day in June. On completion day, I was waiting at our new home and Gerry was overseeing the loading of his furniture into the removal van prior to joining me. The move hit a snag – the monies from the sale of his buyers house were held up by the bank as they were from overseas and had been referred to their money laundering department for investigation. His buyers were sitting outside the flat with their furniture van, his furniture was packed and the van ready to go but despite frantic phone calls between the solicitors and the banks involved, the move was off for that day as the banks stop transferring money after 3.30! I drove home to my room in

Peacehaven bitterly disappointed and Gerry, having seen all his furniture taken off to a depot overnight, spent the night on his sister's sofa. The next day, happily, the money came through once the bank were satisfied we were not part of an international money laundering gang and we got the keys to our new home.

We soon discovered the limitations of our new home. On one side, we were hardly aware of a very quiet neighbour, but on the other side, there lived a man who was at home all day and gave guitar lessons. One of Gerry's favourite pieces of music is 'Hotel California' but there are limits to the number of times you want to hear a student learning to play it, especially that long solo at the end, and it was often quite painful to hear. It seemed to be the only practice piece in the repertoire so there was no relief from it! We could also hear every movement though the thin walls, day and night.

On happier note, we had arranged for the wedding ceremony and reception to be conducted at an old established seafront hotel in the best part of Eastbourne. Gerry had bought me the most beautiful wedding dress and it was the first time I had ever worn such lovely clothes. He also hired a vintage car to take me from Peacehaven to the hotel which was a lovely idea but did not altogether go as planned. My daughters Olga and Vita had done a lot of work applying my makeup and seeing to my hair as I got ready for the journey and I was feeling like a queen as we set out. I soon became rather uncomfortable, as although vintage cars make good photographs they are not the last word in comfort and this one seemed to find every pothole in the road to our destination. Not only that, the driver seemed to take more interest in looking at me in his mirror rather than keeping his eyes on the road, which was something I had to tell him about. When we reached the hotel he parked by the imposing entrance and got out to go round and open my door as I was sitting in the back. As he did so, the car, being on an incline, started to gently roll forward and was about to hit the car in front, when the driver hurriedly reached in just in time and grabbed the handbrake. It could have been so much worse if there had not been a car parked in front as we might have been heading for the cliff top otherwise. I overcame my initial fright and made my way into the hotel, escorted by my daughters, and into the room where the ceremony was taking place, to the strains of Mozart's 'Elvira Madigan' piano concerto.. It was a small occasion, just my children and their partners and Gerry's sisters and their partners plus a few other people but it was a lovely day and after the ceremony we went outside to the lawns where we had photographs taken by a very professional lady we had hired for the day. She later assembled a beautiful album and we also had a memory stick of all the photos. Many of these I put together on my social media page with the title 'Under God's Umbrella' which was how I felt about it. After that we had a separate function room where we were served with our food and wine and had a lovely evening, which came to an end all too soon.

We left the young people to carry on at the bar as long as they liked and Gerry left an open tab. The next morning he had a shock when paying the bill and realised he had seriously underestimated the drinking capacity of my children.

Two of our wedding guests were my son Sergei and his partner Victoria. After all the troubles of his early years he had found good employment as a scaffolder in Germany and we were in fairly regular contact by phone. I was delighted that he was able to come to our wedding and I must say he made a winning impression, particularly with Gerry's sisters, who found him absolutely charming.   He had always had those personable qualities that win people over and never more so than on such an occasion as this. The next morning we all came down to breakfast in varying stages of liveliness and after that we went our separate ways. Sergei and Victoria came back with us as their return flight was the next day. We spent a pleasant day with them and went to bed quite early as I had to go back to work the next day, leaving them to it. I left for work at around 5am while later Gerry would drive them to Gatwick Airport for their flight home.

I had a lovely day at work, everyone offered their congratulations and I came home happy but tired.

We kept a cold drinks cabinet which was always well stocked with various bottles and cans, beers, wines and spirits and I fancied a pick me up. Opening the door, I had a shock as just white space awaited me – it was completely empty. I called Gerry to come and see and we were both lost for words. Obviously my son was like the proverbial leopard and had not changed one bit, despite his charming exterior. Once we got over the shock, we both started laughing at the sheer nerve of what he had done. It's always good to see the funny side of things, although it cost plenty to replenish the missing contents.

I had some weeks holiday left and we decided to go to Cyprus on a belated honeymoon and booked a ten day all inclusive package. We had a lovely hotel, the food was excellent and the sun shone on us every day. It was such a happy experience that we could not wait to go back again but we were starting to wonder about our future plans. My work had become less important to me, we were not entirely happy about where we lived and to cap it all, shortly after moving there I had made an unwelcome discovery. The bungalow opposite the back of our house looked familiar and I realised to my horror that it was indeed the place where I had stayed many a night in the months before I met Gerry. Our arrival had not gone unnoticed because my former dating partner spent a lot of time standing in his garden looking up at our bedroom window. On my birthday, he also left a card and a note under my car's windscreen wipers. This was very unsettling and was another reason for us to look at alternatives. As for my work, I developed a condition on my foot known as *plantar fasciitis* which made it very difficult to walk and was very painful as I was on my feet most of the day.

We now knew that we wanted a detached, or at best, semi detached property and a decent size garden was also a necessity. We both wanted the latter although Gerry had lived in a flat for ten years or so he missed his garden and I wanted to be able to grow vegetables and have plenty of outdoor space. We started looking back in the Eastbourne area but properties in our price range were no more suitable than what we had.

At the same time, I had to go back to Latvia to check up on my flat and settle any bills that might have arisen since my last visit. This was early October and the weather was turning cold there but Gerry fell in love with Madona at first sight. He was taken with the peace and quiet, the nearby lakes and forests and I suppose most of all, the fact that property such as we were interested in, was readily affordable. I arranged for us to look at various properties that were for sale and we were disappointed that they all had serious defects that ruled them out. The last house we looked at was a different matter. It was large detached house with ample gardens surrounding it, a greenhouse and a large basement area that had huge potential. The asking price was such that we would have plenty of spare cash left over from the sale of our house in Bognor and we both agreed that we should buy it. A deal was struck with the owners and we went back to England excited at the prospect of anew adventure together.

We put our house on the market and the agents very soon found us a buyer at the asking price so it was all systems go. We had already booked a second holiday in Cyprus on the strength of how much we had enjoyed the previous one. This time we explored more of the facilities beyond the hotel and found so many wonderful restaurants and cafes that we were spoilt for choice. The weather was still good but the hotel was noticeably quieter and this time we had an assigned spot with our sun loungers next to the pool. I am not the world's greatest swimmer but compared to my husband I was Olympic standard. He had never learnt to swim but was willing to give it a try. Despite my best efforts to encourage him, he could never manage to lift his feet off the bottom of the pool while clinging to his rubber ring. His valiant efforts made me laugh so much I probably involuntarily increased the volume of water in the pool, but at least he tried. On our last day, waiting for the bus to take us to the airport, it started to rain and the wind had picked up. Even in Cyprus, the summer was over.

We now had only a few weeks to tie up all our affairs in England and it was frantic. We had our furniture transported to Latvia in advance as the sellers were quite happy for it to be stored in their house pending our arrival and we managed to sell or dispose of things we did not want to take with us, so that on December 5, 2015 the last items of furniture were moved out into the waiting van, we handed over the keys to the estate agents, trusting that the money would go through all right this time and headed for the airport. In our hotel room where we would stay before our early morning flight, we were relieved to be able to access our banking site on the internet and see that the money from the sale had indeed been deposited in our account and we were all set for our new life back in my home country.

CHAPTER 24

Arriving at my flat we needed some sleep as the next day would see a round of visits to various offices to sort out the formalities of registering as permanent residents and for Gerry to get a resident permit. Latvia is very strong on bureaucracy and procedures and we faced a string of tight lipped and authoritarian women (always women) making us fill in forms with impossibly long reference numbers. My married name caused a problem and it had to be Latvianised by changing the spelling and adding an
'a' at the end to make it legal. At the end of it, we got our official forms back having jumped through all the bureaucratic hoops required of us.
Next was the house purchase which was conducted through a notary with all parties present and an interpreter so Gerry would understand at least some of what was going on. It was not normal practice to have a survey of a prospective property carried out in Latvia before buying and this caused him some concern, as did the fact that the concept of joint and several ownership does not exist in Latvia and so we acquired 50% each. To this day, he does not understand the intricacies of property ownership in Latvia which is very different from the law in England. The upshot was that we were now the owners of our des. res. but we needed to have lots of work done inside and out

before we could move in, so it was as well I still owned the flat where we could live until such time as we could move in with all the work completed.

Throughout the previous months I had been constantly bothered by Vladimir, who persistently tried to phone me and send messages, despite my best efforts to block him. He discovered that I had remarried and that we were living in Madona which was not surprising as word soon gets around in a small town. One evening at about 11pm after Gerry had gone to bed and was asleep, but I was still up, there was a quiet knock on the door, much like the woman in the flat on our landing usually did. Thinking it was her, I opened the door and there stood Vladimir with a large bouquet of flowers in his hand. I told him quietly but forcefully that he had no business knocking on our door and I did not want his flowers. In a drunken rage he hurled them down the stair well and stormed off. A little while later, I saw his mother in the town and she told me that one day he had been brandishing his father's butcher's knife and threatening to kill me. She told me she had taken it away from him and told him not to be so stupid but he said he was going to kill me anyway, with his bare hands if necessary.

In preparation for the work on the house – we needed new windows, new flooring, a new staircase and a lot of painting and decorating I contacted a builder I knew who I thought was reliable and arranged for him to carry out all the works required and a starting date was agreed for the new year. He lived with his wife and child in an apartment block next to ours. One night there was a loud banging on the door, accompanied by shouting and swearing. It was Vladimir again, completely off his head with drink. I phoned our builder and he was there in a minute, thankfully able to persuade Vladimir to go away quietly, otherwise he would call the police.

Work began on the house in the new year and virtually everything needed replacing so we had the best quality triple glazed windows installed, new floor tiles and lots of replastering and painting. We spent most of our spare time going round the DIY warehouses and furniture stores choosing tiles, doors, bathroom suites, white goods and anything else that took our fancy. One day we met a couple in one of the stores where the man's broad accent gave him away, to my husband at least, recognising him as an English northerner. We started to speak and became friends, although we lived quite a long way apart.

We went to the house almost every day to see what progress was being made and one day we went into the garage to have a look round. As we left, Gerry closed the door behind me and I heard a yelp of pain. He had mistaken the door for a simple up and over, whereas it was a roller shutter door and he had the tips of his fingers caught in one of the rollers. My first reaction was to laugh, until I saw the blood! We went quickly to the hospital where his fingers were stitched but to this day he has little or no feeling in the two fingers badly affected.

All was going well with the house and it was gradually nearing the stage when we could move in when it was discovered that the roof was in a very bad way and would likely not withstand the rigours of the forthcoming winter. This was a set back but it had to be done so there was no choice. Something else was to have the sewage and water connected to the mains drainage which was also a necessity and obviously a great improvement on before. We were also able to start working on the garden. The greenhouse was my special pleasure and I was able to harvest more than one hundred buckets of tomatoes in our first year. We bought many young cherry trees, apple trees and a variety of currant bushes, a project for the future. It was an exciting time and we really enjoyed working together in the fresh air of a glorious summer. I introduced Gerry to the delights of berry picking in the forest but he was not very productive, managing half a litre to my seven. In addition, he was badly bitten by the insects in the forest. I applied the usual Latvian remedy of a green alcohol based spirit, resulting in him sporting a multitude of green spots, so much so that I called him my little frog. That first year he was also badly bitten while working in the garden. His English flesh was obviously a tasty novelty for the Latvian insect population who were out in force that summer.

We had a lot of clearing up to do in the house and outside. The old owners had two dogs and it was evident that they never cleaned up after them as there was dog mess everywhere you stepped in the garden so that was one of my less pleasant tasks. Towards the bottom of the garden we had a brick fireplace ideal for barbecues but also for burning rubbish. The previous owners left a great deal of stuff behind which they never came back to collect, so we burnt as much of it as we could including a stack of pornographic magazines. The rest we had to pay someone to take away. One of the little peculiarities of life in Latvia is that builders and workmen in general never dispose of their waste after they have finished the job, an annoying fact that Gerry could never get used to. After the building and redecoration was finished we were left with a whole load of rubbish to dispose of. Vladimir still bothered me from time to time but now his tone was pleading rather than threatening. He had no job, there was no money for food and such like. I gave him the chance to come to our house and clean up some of the mess left in the garden, which was mainly lots of timber left over by the builder together with cutting down some dead trees. We let him loose with the chainsaw and to be fair, he was doing a very good job. He built a neat log store at the bottom of the garden and we were very pleased with his work, although he had not finished what he was being paid to do. I fed him during the week and gave him food to take home as well. We had arranged to go to England for a long weekend as Gerry's sisters and cousins were having a reunion meeting in Eastbourne. While we were away we also had some work arranged in the garden to dig a soakaway for the water from the drainpipes, which otherwise had nowhere to go and was liable to cause flooding in the event of heavy rain. While we were away I had a phone call from the builder to tell me that Vladimir was drunk and trying to lord it over them while they were working. Once again he had broken my trust and was told to go home.

CHAPTER 25

Life that summer was wonderful. We were in our new house and so pleased with it, although it had cost us as much to refurbish as it had to buy it. We had a lovely new wooden staircase, a fitted kitchen and lots of other things to enjoy. We had a large basement which apart from a boiler room and a place to store our wooden pellets for the central heating system had plenty of room to one day have a sauna and shower room built. Most important of all, there was a large cold room which had ample space for me to store all the pickled and preserved food I would eventually put in jars to keep for the winter, tomatoes, cucumbers, apple juice and other juices made from the fruits of our own orchard.

The only cloud on the horizon was the result of the Brexit referendum in the UK. We had not taken this factor into account when we moved to Latvia as it seemed unlikely at the time that the 'vote leave' campaigners would get their way. However when the news came through in June 2016 that Britain was going to leave the EU we were shocked. The implications of this were not fully understood at the time, but we knew that our situation might cause problems. In particular, what would happen to me if the borders were suddenly closed and I could not go to England? What would happen if Gerry, who was in his seventies, died and I wanted to go to England to be near my children, three of whom lived there?   What would his status be if anything happened to me?   No one knew the answers and the lengthy period of negotiation only prolonged the agony as to what were we to do.   In the end we decided to carry on as normal until things were made a little clearer but from then on it was always at the back of our minds.

That summer went by too fast, like summers usually do, but we had some good times.   At the back of the house, at ground floor level, we had a long balcony with steps leading down to the garden.   Having sold my flat, I spent some of the money on my dream, which was to have a series of lamps and lampposts around the garden.   On warm summer evenings we could sit out on the balcony with friends and enjoy food from our barbecue and some drinks, switch on the lights as the daylight faded and bask in the luxury of it.   It all seemed a far cry from that one room flat in a wooden barn and it meant everything to me to share it with my husband and my friends.

Friend is a word that is used much too casually.   To me a friend is a soulmate, someone as close as a family member, someone you would do anything to help and someone who would do the same for you.   Someone to rely on, someone to turn to in times of trouble and someone who is always on your side.

Anna was my friend.   We had first met when I returned to Latvia from my Siberian adventure, a chance encounter on the street where we were near neighbours. I got to know her gradually and we got in the habit of having a coffee together some mornings and maybe a few drinks at weekends. I was on my own and she had problems at home. Her husband was an ex army officer who had been stationed at the Russian barracks at Marciena. He suffered a bad motorcycle accident, fracturing his skull. Although he was not expected to live, after he was operated on he did survive but had suffered brain damage. He was discharged from the army but only received a small disability pension. His moods were erratic and he often made no sense. They had a son who I disliked - a lazy, dishonest boy given to thieving and thoroughly spoilt by his mother, whom he could twist round his little finger. Anna, an accomplished machinist, worked at a textiles factory where they made bespoke articles of clothing like jumpers to order from a pattern book as well as curtains and other household goods.

Big changes were afoot in the Soviet bloc at this time. Gorbachev's perestroika had began a thaw in the icy grip held by Russia on its constituent republics and the strikes in the Polish shipyards fuelled demands for independence. Other Soviet republics also began agitating for their own freedom. In 1989, Estonia, Latvia and Lithuania had formed the Baltic Way, a human chain of 600 kilometres which stretched from Riga to Vilnius and expressed the Baltic republics unified desire to be independent nations again. Finally, this was granted in September 1991.

Much as this was celebrated in a burst of nationalist pride, the economic consequences were initially disastrous. It took until 2004 for Latvia to be admitted to the European Union and in the intervening period many businesses, having lost their principal market, exports to Russia, went to the wall. Madona, although only a small town, had many varied and successful businesses which provided employment for the population, but within a short time it lost its electrical factory where I had worked, its mink and silver fox farms. The farmers found that there was nowhere to sell their produce, be it crops or livestock. Inevitably, Anna's factory was another of the casualties. With only her husband's disability allowance as income, the family were soon clocking up debts and had no money to buy even essential food items. One day she failed to turn up for our now regular coffee mornings and I discovered that her husband had collapsed as he had no food the previous day. From then on, I started cooking for them as well as my own family, in fact as far as I was concerned, they were my family too and I made sure they always had enough food to eat. I was also able to let them have clothes for free from my stock as they were in such a desperate state. We had some very happy times together. One day we went to my mother's for her birthday and having had a few drinks too many, had to be helped home by her husband, one of us on each arm, as although he was brain damaged, was still a very strong man.

After about a year of this, her husband was found a job he could do helping out in the forest. Not cutting down any trees of course, but as a general helper fetching and carrying things which given his strength was ideal for him. The local authority had by now devised a scheme whereby homeless or unemployed people could offset their household bills by performing community service in the town such as tending flower beds, sweeping the streets etc. and Anna was able to do this, which helped their situation. I had been only to happy to help them in the ways I have described, without thought of repayment or reward because I regarded her as my friend, So it was with some shock and disbelief that one Friday evening, looking out of my window I saw her and her husband carrying bags which contained cakes and champagne bottles. Not for me, but for a woman that she had been working with in the town and with whom she had struck up a friendship.

The next time I saw her I confronted her face to face about what I saw as a betrayal on her part to which she answered that she was sorry and hadn't realised how it appeared on my side. Although we remained on friendly terms after this, something had been lost that could never be replaced, and sadly, it was not the last time I was left disillusioned by her actions.

Despite that, through the years we always stayed in touch so that when I returned to Madona in 2015 she was one of the first people to get in touch and once again we met regularly. When we moved into our new house she became a frequent visitor together with her man friend Eric. We had many pleasant meals together as we did with other friends of mine from the old days.

In 2019, I turned sixty and my children got together to pay for a holiday in Crete. Olga, Vita and Vitaly and their respective partners together with me and Gerry had a very enjoyable ten days in the sun with good food and drink in an excellent hotel. It was only marred by my husband's bad sunburn. He went to sleep in the sun one afternoon soon after we arrived and neglected to cover his lower legs and feet. For the rest of our time there he was hobbling around in great pain and to make matters worse, the doctor he saw prescribed pills which meant he was off alcohol for the duration.

Back home it was now becoming clear that in December 2020 England was going to pull up the drawbridge and if we wanted to go back there we had to do something about it fairly soon. For the reasons I have said, we really had no choice but to return to the UK thinking long term so we put the house on the market. There was little or no interest as the months ticked away and soon our options had shrunk down to the possibilities of renting a flat pending the eventual sale of our house. In the early months of 2020 our problems were compounded by the outbreak of Covid-19. Latvia went into lockdown as did everywhere else and we could not fly to England to view any possible accommodation. As things started to ease after the first wave, by June thanks to Vita's efforts we managed to arrange a tenancy of a flat in Eastbourne, albeit without actually seeing it and were able to fly to England in July having sent some of our essential belongings ahead. Our good friend Lucettte kindly picked us up at the airport and drove us to our new home and having been up most of the previous night in order to get to Riga airport for our early morning flight, we were glad to get to bed after sorting out a few essentials, like making sure the internet and the television were in working order. The flat itself left a lot to be desired, the kitchen was tiny and the shower room was not exactly luxurious but the living room was ok and so was the bedroom. There was another room which Gerry could use as his office as he was still involved in producing a monthly on line music magazine, which he had been doing for the last twenty years and was not about to give up now. The next morning we discovered that the lock on the front door was jammed and we were effectively locked in. This was not the introduction we had been looking forward to and we were fortunate that we could get a locksmith in to deal with it as promptly as he did.

The most important thing now was for me to get settled status so that I would have no trouble remaining in England after the shutters came down and this was achieved in a surprisingly short time thanks to the help we had from Lucette, who guided us through the application form.

Having achieved that, all we could do was try to get my medical problems sorted out. I have type two diabetes, high blood pressure and constant muscular pain from spinal degeneration and over the next few months I had many consultations with various specialists, and my treatment is ongoing. I am not a political person, but having seen how hard the staff work to treat their patients, especially in these covid affected times, I can bear witness that the NHS is a wonderful institution and long may it continue and not be picked off by private health companies looking for profit.

The covid pandemic continues and our lives, like everyone else's, have been dramatically affected by the restrictions we are living under. My story is up to date but my journey is unfinished. As I write we are facing a dilemma. Do we return to our lovely house in Madona and pick up where we left off? In many ways we would be happy to do so. Do we stay on in this rented flat which is draining our finances every month while we try to keep two homes going in the hope that eventually someone will buy our house? Choices will have to be made sooner rather than later and I know, and now the reader does too, that I have not made the wisest choice every time I was faced with a fork in the road. All I know is that regrets are a waste of time and that we have to look forward to the future and not harp back to the past. Together with my husband, we will go forward to whatever awaits us, wherever that might be, but the journey still has a long way to go.

POSTSCRIPT

We returned to Latvia to live comfortably in our fine house and lovely gardens after a year in England draining our finances as well as the attendant covid related restrictions making life difficult. Pent up in a flat with no outside space. A hard winter ensued and as I write, the Russian invasion of Ukraine has begun, casting dark clouds over the future here.

Life goes on but the road ahead is no doubt still full of unknown twists and turns as it ever was and will always be.

Printed in Great Britain
by Amazon